INTEGRAL BUDDHISM
Developing All Aspects
of One's Personhood

Books by Traleg Kyabgon

King Doha: Saraha's Advice to a King, Shogam Publications, 2018

Letter to a Friend: Nagarjuna's Classic Text, Shogam Publications, 2018

Song of Karmapa: The Aspiration of the Mahamudra of True Meaning by Lord Rangjung Dorje, Shogam Publications, 2018

Moonbeams of Mahamudra: The Classic Meditation Manual, Shogam Publications, 2015

Karma: What it is, What it isn't, and Why it matters, Shambhala Publications, 2015

Four Dharmas of Gampopa, KTD Publications, 2013

Asanga's Abhidharmasamuccaya, KTD Publications, 2013

Ninth Karmapa Wangchuk Dorje's Ocean Of Certainty, KTD Publications, 2011

Influence of Yogacara on Mahamudra, KTD Publications, 2010

The Practice of Lojong: Cultivating Compassion through Training the Mind, Shambhala Publications, 2007

Mind at Ease: Self-Liberation through Mahamudra Meditation, Shambhala Publications, 2004

Benevolent Mind: A Manual in Mind Training, Zhyisil Chokyi Ghatsal Publications, 2003

The Essence of Buddhism: An Introduction to Its Philosophy and Practice, Shambhala Publications, 2002 & 2014

Photo facing page: Traleg Kyabgon Rinpoche the Ninth

INTEGRAL BUDDHISM
Developing All Aspects of One's Personhood

Traleg Kyabgon

Foreword by Dzigar Kongtrül Rinpoche

SHOGAM
PUBLICATIONS
2018

Shogam Publications Pty Ltd
PO Box 239 Ballarat, Victoria, Australia, 3353
www.shogam.org
info@shogam.com

Copyright © 2018 Felicity Lodro
First Edition

All rights reserved. No part of this publication may be reproduced in any form or by any means electronic or mechanical, including photocopying, recording, or by any information storage and retrieval system without prior permission in writing from the publisher. Enquiries should be made to the publisher.

Shogam Publications Pty Ltd has made every effort to contact the copyright holder of all material not owned by the publisher reproduced herein, interested parties may contact the publisher for further information.

Printed in Australia and the United States of America

Edited by Salvatore Celiento
Designed by David Bennett

National Library of Australia
Kyabgon, Traleg, 1955
Integral Buddhism: Developing all Aspects Of One's Personhood

Printed book ISBN: 978-0-6481148-0-2 (paperback)
E-book ISBN: 978-0-6481148-1-9

DEDICATION

Dedicated to all mother sentient beings who at one time, cradled us with great loving kindness and compassion

Contents

Foreword by Dzigar Kongtrül Rinpoche ... x
Biography of Author ... xi
Acknowledgements ... xiv
Editor's Introduction ... xv
Editor's Biography ... xvii

SECTION 1: INTEGRAL BUDDHISM

1. Towards an Integral Buddhist View ... 1
2. An Integral Approach to Meditation ... 6
   Unlocking Our Resources ... 7
   Using the Breath in Meditation ... 8
   Mindfulness ... 11
   Overcoming Obstacles in Meditation ... 14
   Esoteric Meditation ... 19
   Integral Meditation ... 20
3. Integral Buddhism, Ignorance, and Suffering ... 21
   Self and Personhood ... 25
   Four noble truths, Ethics, and the Integral Approach ... 28
   Ethics ... 31
4. The Integral Approach to Overcoming Suffering ... 33
   Misunderstanding and Excessive Mental Reflection ... 35
   Pursuing an Integral Approach ... 38

Renunciation	42
Mindfulness, Awareness, and Thinking Clearly	44

5. Working with Suffering and Becoming Stronger — 45
   - *Three Kinds of Suffering* — 46
   - *Craving and Desire* — 47
   - *Desire, Freedom, and Renunciation* — 48
   - *Self-Identity* — 51
   - *Merit and Wisdom* — 52
   - *Ego and Personality* — 53
   - *Transformation* — 54
   - *Courage, Strength, Fortitude, Resilience* — 56

6. Noble Eightfold Path — 58

7. Foundations of Wisdom — 63
   - *Craving, Beauty, and Dharmas* — 64
   - *Interrelationship and Is-ness* — 67
   - *Fixation and Misunderstanding* — 68
   - *Mindfulness and Interdependent Origination* — 69
   - *Wisdom* — 73

SECTION 2. PHILOSOPHY

8. Why Integrate Philosophy? — 74
   - *Values* — 76

9. Abhidharma (Pali: Abhidhamma) — 78
   - *Hinayana* — 83
   - *Hinayana and Mahayana* — 83

10. Yogacara — 87

11. Madhyamaka — 93
    - *Fixation* — 97

12. Madhyamaka, Emptiness, and Compassion — 98
    - *Interdependent Arising and Compassion* — 100

Middle View	102
Bodhicitta and Becoming a Bodhisattva	104
13. Mahayana, Bodhicitta, and Six Paramitas	110
Six Paramitas	111
The Integral Approach to Philosophy	115

SECTION 3: PSYCHOLOGY

14. Psychology, Spirituality, and the Mind	119
Understanding Our Mind	120
Meditation	122
Acceptance	124
Attraction and Aversion	126
Misunderstanding	126
Letting Go and Sense of Self	130
Spirituality and Psychology	132
Contextualizing of the Self	133
Integral Psychology	136

SECTION 4: HEALTH AND WELL-BEING

15. Prana and Pranayama	138
Prana	142
Prana, Nadi, and Chakras	147
Five Primary Pranas	149
Five Secondary Pranas	151
16. Tibetan Medicine	155
Bile (Tib. Tripa)	156
Phlegm (Tib. Peken)	157
Causes of Malfunction and Recommended Actions	159
Integral Approach to Health	163
17. Conclusion	165
Notes	167
Index	177

Foreword

Traleg Rinpoche was a great teacher and a good friend of mine. He inspired me and many others, demonstrating with his own life how an authentic Tibetan teacher from such a different culture and upbringing could adapt completely to Western society and surroundings, yet at the same time remain deeply rooted in his own genuine dharmic culture and wisdom tradition. This book of Rinpoche's is a portrait of himself. It shows how Western and modern dharma students can use the teachings and the path of meditation to shape our core values and beliefs while remaining fluid in the world we live, with no conflict.

Meditation practice, however great it is, must be integrated with the daily lives of individuals and their culture. If not, it becomes disconnected and separate from life. That is not how the great masters of the past, including Traleg Rinpoche, lived. Here Rinpoche gives deep insight into how we can be creative yet remain traditional; how we can be wise, but also practical for our time and present-day needs; and how we can socially integrate these teachings into our larger world.

I deeply appreciate such books as this. Rather than watering down the dharma, it makes it shine more brightly in our diverse world and rapidly changing time, where we all need many ways to approach our lives. I also deeply appreciate Traleg Khandro and all of Rinpoche's students who are putting so much effort into ensuring that his teachings continually bring great benefit to the world. By assembling and producing his teachings into book form, they allow his profound wisdom and skillful means to reach us all. In this way Rinpoche's legacy continues, and its benefit continues as well.

Dzigar Khontrül Rinpoche

Biography of Author
TRALEG KYABGON RINPOCHE IX

Traleg Kyabgon Rinpoche IX (1955-2012) was born in Nangchen in Kham, eastern Tibet. He was recognized by His Holiness XVI Gyalwang Karmapa as the ninth Traleg tulku and enthroned at the age of two as the supreme abbot of Thrangu Monastery. Rinpoche was taken to Rumtek Monastery in Sikkim at the age of four where he was educated with other young tulkus in exile by His Holiness Karmapa for the next five years.

Rinpoche began his studies under the auspices of His Eminence Kyabje Thuksey Rinpoche at Sangngak Choling in Darjeeling. He also studied with a number of other eminent Tibetan teachers during that time and mastered the many Tibetan teachings with the Kagyü and Nyingma traditions in particular including the *Hevajra Tantra*, *Guhyasamaja Tantra*, and the third Karmapa's *Zabmo Nangdon* (*The Profound Inner Meaning*) under Khenpo Noryang (abbot of Sangngak Choling). Rinpoche studied the *Abhidharmakosha*, *Pramanavarttika*, *Bodhisattvacharyavatara*, *Abhidharmasamuccaya*, *Six Treaties of Nagarjuna*, the *Madhyantavibhaga*, and the *Mahayanuttaratantra* with Khenpo Sogyal. He also studied with Khenpo Sodar and was trained in tantric ritual practices by Lama Ganga, who had been specifically sent by His Holiness Karmapa for that purpose.

In 1967 Rinpoche moved to the Institute of Higher Tibetan Studies in Sarnath, and studied extensively for the next five years. He studied Buddhist history, Sanskrit, and Hindi, as well as Longchenpa's *Finding Comfort and Ease* (*Ngalso Korsum*), *Seven Treasuries* (*Longchen Dzod Dun*), *Three Cycles of Liberation* (*Rangdrol Korsum*), and *Longchen Nyingthig* with Khenchen Palden Sherab Rinpoche and Khenpo Tsondru.

When Rinpoche had completed these studies at the age of sixteen, he was sent by His Holiness Karmapa to study under the auspices of the Venerable Khenpo Yeshe Chodar at Sanskrit University in Varanasi for three years. Rinpoche was also tutored by khenpos and geshes from all four traditions of Tibetan Buddhism during this time.

Rinpoche was subsequently put in charge of Zangdog Palri Monastery (the glorious copper colored mountain) in Eastern Bhutan and placed under the private tutelage of Dregung Khenpo Ngedon by His Holiness Karmapa to continue his studies of Sutra and Tantra. He ran this monastery for the next three years and began learning English during this time.

From 1977 to 1980, Rinpoche returned to Rumtek in Sikkim to fill the honored position of His Holiness' translator, where he dealt with many English-speaking Western visitors.

Rinpoche moved to Melbourne, Australia in 1980 and commenced studies in religion and philosophy at LaTrobe University. Rinpoche established E-Vam Institute in Melbourne in 1982 and went on to establish further Centers in Australia, America and New Zealand. For the next 25 years Rinpoche gave weekly teachings, intensive weekend courses, and retreats on classic Kagyu and Nyingma texts. During this time Rinpoche also taught internationally travelling extensively through America, Europe, and South East Asia and was appointed the Spiritual Director of Kamalashila Institute in Germany for five years in the 1980s.

Rinpoche established a retreat center, Maitripa Centre in Healesville, Australia in 1997 where he conducted two public retreats a year. Rinpoche founded E-Vam Buddhist Institute in the US in 2000, and Nyima Tashi Buddhist Centre in New Zealand 2004. In 2010 Rinpoche established a Buddhist college called Shogam Vidhalaya at E-Vam Institute in Australia and instructed students on a weekly basis.

Throughout his life Rinpoche gave extensive teachings on many aspects of Buddhist psychology and philosophy, as well as comparative religion, and Buddhist and Western thought. He was an active writer and has many titles to his name. Titles include: the best selling *Essence of Buddhism*; *Karma, What It Is, What It Isn't, and Why It Matters*; *The Practice of Lojong*; *Moonbeams of Mahamudra*; and many more. Many of Rinpoche's books are translated into a number of different languages including Chinese, French, German, Korean, and Spanish. Rinpoche's writings are thought provoking, challenging, profound, and highly relevant to today's world and its many challenges.

Rinpoche was active in publishing during the last two decades of his life, beginning with his quarterly magazine *Ordinary Mind* which ran from 1997 to 2003. Further, Rinpoche founded his own publishing arm Shogam Publications in 2008 and released a number of books on Buddhist history, philosophy, and psychology and left instructions for the continuation of this vision. His vision for Shogam and list of titles can be found at www.shogam.com.

Rinpoche's ecumenical approach can be seen in his other activities aimed at bringing Buddhadharma to the West. He established the biannual Buddhism and Psychotherapy Conference (1994 - 2003), and Tibet Here and Now Conference (2005), and the annual Buddhist Summer School (1984 to the present).

Traleg Kyabgon Rinpoche IX passed into parinirvana on 24 July 2012, on Chokhor Duchen, the auspicious day of the Buddha's first teaching. Rinpoche stayed in meditation (*thugdam*) for weeks after his passing. A traditional cremation ceremony was conducted at Maitripa Centre and a stupa was erected on the center's grounds in Rinpoche's honor.

It is a privilege to continue to release the profound teachings of Traleg Kyabgon Rinpoche IX given in the West for over 30 years. Rinpoche's Sangha hope that many will benefit.

Acknowledgements

First and foremost, so many thanks must go to the unsurpassed Traleg Kyabgon Rinpoche IX for giving us the precious gift of these teachings. This work would not have been possible without Traleg Khandro, for her deep insight into Rinpoche's teachings, Lyn Hutchison for her skill in Sanskrit and Tibetan, David Bennett for creating the beautiful cover and formatting the work, and Claire Blaxell for her profound command of English. Thank you to Kathleen Gregory for guidance in editing these teachings. May all beings benefit.

Salvatore Celiento

Editor's Introduction

The precious teachings presented here by Traleg Kyabgon Rinpoche the Ninth represent a shift from his previous teaching style. While an extensive record exists of Rinpoche making commentaries on traditional texts, the teachings found in this book share the spontaneous outpouring of wisdom from Rinpoche's heart towards the last two years of his life. Rinpoche focused on integral Buddhism during this time, believing it to be a very important approach. These teachings represent a culmination of particular issues, misunderstandings, and concerns of the Western student of Buddhism and also demonstrate a reframing or reconstruction of traditional Buddhism within the contemporary context while keeping true to tradition, and at the same time being relevant to our modern lives.

Rinpoche noticed that musicians, artists, and indeed, people with passions and interests spent less time with, or even renounced, these passions once they started to practice Buddhism. In these teachings, it is made clear that music, arts and crafts, physical exercise, yoga, breath work, psychology, philosophy, meditation, science, and indeed, whatever is beneficial to oneself and others is Dharma practice.

As an editor of these teachings, the impact on my personal spiritual journey has been profound. Rinpoche's teachings on an integrated path to Buddhism have allowed my previously parallel paths of music, martial arts, yoga, and painting to be conceptually reframed and integrated as a single path of Dharma, as opposed to being separate and distinct activities. In Rinpoche's words:

"According to Buddhism, every time we are doing something that benefits us in a proper way, this is a Dharma practice. Anything that we do that is detrimental to our well-being, is non-dharma or non-dharmic."

Rinpoche is not overly explicit in defining the integral approach to Buddhism, but rather, takes us on a journey, showing us and pointing the way to Buddhist practice and philosophy that encompasses whatever is beneficial, integrating the many human pursuits towards the short-term goal of happiness and the long-term one of enlightenment.

Salvatore Celiento
Editor
Shogam Publications

Editor's Biography

Salvatore Celiento has lectured on counseling in universities in Australia for many years and was accepted to study as a Shedra student by Traleg Kyabgon Rinpoche IX in 2010. He has completed 7 years of a 10 year Shedra program, studying traditional texts from the Kagyü and Nyingma Schools of Tibetan Buddhism. Salvatore has a degree in Pastoral Counseling from Australian Catholic University and Master's degree in Counseling from Victoria University in Australia. He is an accomplished martial artist in the Japanese tradition of Ninjutsu. His other studies include the Shakuhachi bamboo flute (with Grandmaster Riley Lee), Tibetan Yoga, and Japanese brush painting.

INTEGRAL BUDDHISM
Developing All Aspects
of One's Personhood

Section One

Integral Buddhism

1
Towards an Integral Buddhist View

The integral approach of Buddhism involves looking comprehensively at the human condition, at human well-being. It should not be thought of as only addressing certain isolated issues of personal welfare. People may have the tendency to think in that way. Some may think of Buddhism as a religion, others may think of it as a form of spiritual path, and increasingly in the modern world, yet others may see Buddhism as a form of psychology or psychotherapy. Traditionally however, Buddhism is seen as encompassing all aspects of the human condition and existence, not just one single aspect. For example, if you go to a Tibetan doctor, that doctor is not just a practitioner of the Tibetan form of medicine. The very medicine they practice is founded on Buddhist philosophy and psychology. This is the interesting part about Buddhism. Even if we learn to do Buddhist yoga practices, these teachings are also founded on Buddhist principles of the body-mind complex of health and well-being.

Buddhism should not be thought of purely as a philosophy, a form of religion or spirituality, or just a technique to help one deal with one's mind, with mental problems. It is worthwhile asking,

"How has Buddhism been understood by people living in Buddhist countries and people brought up as Buddhists?" For example, in Tibetan Buddhism, we do not think of Buddhism as just a philosophy, a system of psychology, a form of spirituality, or a religion, as previously stated. Traditionally, if you study Buddhism, medicine, art and craft, or linguistics, and so on, these pursuits are considered extensions of one's interest in the Dharma[1] and an extension of one's pursuit of knowledge. From the Buddhist point of view, if knowledge is pursued effectively, it is regarded as positive because Buddhism is designed to bring illumination. Buddhism explains, "The reason we suffer and find our life unsatisfactory, why there is so much dissatisfaction, is because we are shrouded in ignorance of our true nature and the true nature of things."

In Buddhist countries, Buddhism is seen as encompassing many aspects and dimensions of the human experience, and not as a singular entity. Such misinterpretation has accompanied the spread of Buddhism to the Western world. For example, some argue that the Buddhist practices of mindfulness and meditation are helpful, but Buddhist theoretical ideas have little merit. Others maintain that modern science is the ultimate authority on reality and Buddhism's approach to reality is useless, and thus we should not try to understand Buddhist psychology or philosophy.

I want to emphasize that, on the contrary, we can learn a lot from Buddhism. When I look at Western psychology, philosophy, and even theology, and then the Buddhist tradition and Buddhist thought, I do not find Buddhist thought to be lacking in any way. It ranks highly in terms of its profundity. Buddhist thinking does not reflect a premodern way of thinking. Nor is the modern view always necessarily good. Just because it is modern, just because it is current, does not mean it is superior to how people thought in the past. This is a major misconception. With the study of Western history, for example, more and more historians are now saying that the Middle Ages in the West were not the "Dark Ages," in the way modern historians and modern thinkers interpreted and portrayed that period.

With the integral approach to Buddhist practice, it includes opportunities to look into our lives in many different ways: dimensionally from a psychological point of view, a philosophical point of view, an ethical point of view, in terms of physical health and well-being, and so on. I will be talking in this book about these many different perspectives, including that of Buddhist medicine, which in Tibetan Buddhism, is very important. So, with the integral approach to Buddhism, all the different aspects of human knowledge, of human pursuits, need to become integrated with one's personal path. This is what is meant by "integral" in this context.

We can still practice Buddhism while integrating modern scientific points of view. The 14th Dalai Lama has taken this approach insofar as he has instituted an annual series of dialogues with scientists such as physicists and neuroscientists, called the "Mind & Life Conferences." He has done this for many years.

It is quite acceptable to incorporate modern theoretical physics into the Buddhist philosophical way of thinking, frame Buddhist teachings and practices of meditation in scientific language, and also, when available, lend scientific weight to any measurable results from Buddhist meditation practices.

The 14th Dalai Lama is very open to such integration, and this is not necessarily a new phenomenon. In the 19th century, there was a movement called the Rimé[2] movement, based on the idea of non-sectarianism. One of the key instigators, the first Jamgon Kongtrul Rinpoche[3] (1813-99), brought a variety of Buddhist philosophies and practices together. He grouped them under the title, the "Eight Chariots." The Eight Chariots of Buddhism included almost everything that we can practice in Buddhism, from very simple mind-training practices, to the most esoteric forms of practice.

In other words, instead of focusing on just one type of practice or one school of thought, the integral approach incorporates whatever is beneficial, helpful, or gives an alternative perspective. Whether it is done in a traditional way or is in a more modern context, like the 14th Dalai Lama's approach, the underlying spirit of integral Buddhism is the same: to integrate, to bring different kinds of practices into the mainstream of Buddhism.

Taking this into consideration, one may ask, "Isn't it true that many traditions advise against mixing paths or traditions because this leads to one not following an authentic path and creates more confusion?" This is a good question. I believe we must have one path[4] that we follow. I do not believe one can follow many paths at the same time. Having the integral approach is like obtaining a suitable selection of provisions for our journey so that we have all kinds of resources to sustain us. But we are still following only one main path. This is important.

To use a cooking metaphor, if one is making pumpkin soup, it has to look like pumpkin soup and taste like pumpkin soup. One can add different ingredients, but they have to work, and they have to enhance the flavor of the pumpkin soup. Whatever one adds to it should not turn it into another soup. This is the danger when we combine many things in equal measure. It ends up not tasting like anything; it is neither one thing, nor the other. Whatever it is that we are cooking, it still has to taste, smell, and look like pumpkin soup, except it has a richer flavor.

We have to perform a balancing act. Being too myopic, too narrow in our focus may not be a good approach to practice but, on the other hand, if we are too open, this is not ideal either. Accordingly, I am not suggesting that we should be completely non-discriminatory in what we incorporate or take on. What is taken on has to blend well with what we are already practicing, what we already believe. We cannot do a copy and paste job. Mixing many different religions is not going to work.

Thus, the integral approach has many levels, bringing different disciplines together; even within one particular tradition or practice, we incorporate many related practices. This is the key point: approaching it from many different angles.

2
An Integral Approach to Meditation

If we look at Tibetan Buddhist meditation practitioners, we will find they do not practice only one type of meditation, and this is very important to remember. The Tibetan system is based on what is called the three *yana*[5] approach to the Buddhist path, yana meaning "vehicle." When we practice the Dharma, we use the teachings as a vehicle to help transport us from the state of samsaric confusion, to the state of liberation, and then to nirvana or enlightenment.

We have the option of choosing from these three kinds of vehicles. After we have reached a particular point on the journey, we can actually abandon this yana, approach, or vehicle, opt for another one, and continue on with the journey. Later on, if we find that vehicle to be unsatisfactory or inadequate, we can still board the one remaining vehicle.

So we can choose from three vehicles to travel to our destination of enlightenment. Based on this principle of the three yanas in Buddhism, we practice accordingly. First, we have the option of doing meditation in a particular way. Then, as we advance a little further, we continue with these practices, but do them in a slightly different way. As we go further, we continue in a similar fashion.

When looking at different types of meditation, they can seem in complete contradiction to each other or may seem to present a very confusing picture of how these meditation practices are to be pursued. However, if we look deeper into the practices, we will see that they are interconnected—all our different practices connect at certain points.

In Buddhism, all practices are reduced to what we call the "three principles of Buddhism."[6] The first one is the conduct aspect: how to live our life in a wholesome way, not "wholesome" in a moralistic sense but, rather, a life that is beneficial and life-enhancing, not destructive to our own welfare and the welfare involving other living beings.

This way of living has to stem from one's practice of meditation (Skt. *bhavana*), which is the second Buddhist principle that we practice. Meditation is designed to produce a mind that is more stable, with a greater capacity to concentrate, and not as scattered and diffuse, as the ground on which wisdom, the third principle, can develop. This is called *samadhi* in Sanskrit. Samadhi is the product of meditation. Sometimes samadhi has been misunderstood to mean "meditation." Rather, samadhi is what we can attain when we practice meditation properly. Simply "doing" meditation may not necessarily lead to having a samadhi experience.

Unlocking Our Resources

According to Buddhism, we have to be more self-reliant in relation to finding fulfillment in our lives and making our lives more meaningful. This is because, fundamentally speaking, as Buddha himself has said, we normally try to find this in two different ways. One is to rush off to find refuge in a greater being, such as the creator of the universe, or to find it in other people. We try to find our happiness and meaning in life through the lives of others.

According to Buddhism, these two cannot be trusted. We cannot have complete faith that a great being is going to protect us from all manner of unwanted and adverse circumstances and situations, nor that the people we hope will love, nurture, and respect us will necessarily do that. What we can rely on is our own abilities, our own wits and resources. Tapping into one's own resources is the key to finding fulfillment in life. If we have this approach, all other relationships can subsequently be founded upon that.

What is the key to unlocking the resources trapped within us? Buddhists believe the key is the practice of meditation. Meditation is seen as extremely important because it is designed to help tap into the reservoir of our hidden talents, energy, enthusiasm, joy, love, and compassion. Freeing these up is what the practice of meditation is supposed to do for us, which is the opposite of what some may understand to be the reason for meditation. They may think meditation is used to suppress and put everything back into the box and clean it up. This is not necessarily the idea.

Of course, there is a cleaning up process that goes on with meditation as well. However, it is not like putting things away and then putting a padlock on it. It is about throwing out that which we do not need, going through everything there, and finding hidden treasures that we did not know were there. We recognize that there is a lot of rubbish so we throw it out. As we throw out more and more rubbish, we begin to find more and more material that we need to keep. Meditation has to be used in that way.

Using the Breath in Meditation

How we practice meditation at the beginning is stated very clearly by the Buddha in his discourse on meditation on breath as the object of meditation, the *Anapanasati Sutta*.[7] There, Buddha describes the practice of meditation using breath. In that sutta, there is a detailed description of how to practice breathing meditation. Right from the beginning, in Buddhism, meditation is practiced in such a way that we are not just using our mind, but using our body as well. The posture is emphasized, breath is emphasized, and then of course, the mind. Even a simple meditation is not to do with thinking about something and trying to cultivate our mind while completely blocking everything out when it comes to our bodily states. The body is incorporated as part of meditation. We actually use the breath to work with our mind.

In Buddhism, and in Indian thought generally, breath is seen as a very important agent. It is seen as a link between life and death, between sentience and non-sentience, and between consciousness and unconsciousness. The breath that we have in relation to exhalation and inhalation is the grosser manifestation of breath. Breath, in essence, is accompanied not only by oxygen but also life energy, called *prana* in Sanskrit. We use breath to harmonize the body and mind. Normally, body and mind are basically working on parallel tracks. The body is going along this way and the mind another way, and there is hardly any correlation between the two. Through focusing on the breath in meditation, and paying more attention to that process, body and mind can become harmonized, in a way. This type of meditation helps one attain a level of ease. One becomes more at ease because the body and mind are working in harmony. Even if they are not in total harmony, at least they become more harmonious.

To begin with, in meditation, when resting our mind, we try not to pay too much attention to what we are thinking. There may be all kinds of superfluous thoughts and feelings, things we are dreaming about, our expectations regarding life generally, or one's thoughts of the immediate future. Rather, we simply try to bring our mind to the present, not allowing different thoughts, feelings, dreams, and so on to be our area of focus. Again, in relation to this, breath is seen as a very useful agent. When we breathe and we pay attention to this, we cannot but be present. When we exhale, we know we are exhaling. When we inhale, we know we are inhaling. We cannot hold onto our breath forever. One has to let go, and then one breathes in and one breathes out.

When we turn our attention to the breath, we are immediately brought into the present. For instance, if we place an object in our visual field and gaze at it, one may only be able to concentrate on it for a very short period of time. Sometimes, the object gradually becomes blurry, or one becomes groggy, or one starts to daydream, and so on. In other words, it is hard to concentrate. In the beginning, if we try to pay attention to our thoughts, feelings, etcetera, we will not be able to easily rest the mind in the present. This is because thoughts and emotions are arising and dissipating, arising and dissipating all the time. This is the reason that breath is used to anchor our attention to the present. By using the breath, we learn to have experience of what it is like to be in the present: one is breathing and not thinking about anything else. The Buddha says we should think, "Now I am breathing out," when we are breathing out. When we are breathing in, one thinks, "Now I am breathing in."

Focusing on the breath and thinking, "I'm breathing in, I'm breathing out," prevents the mind being filled with a range of mundane thoughts—from cooking dinner to picking up the kids. Rather, one is thinking "I am breathing in, I am breathing out. I am breathing in, I am breathing out." While we are engaged in that physical activity of exhalation and inhalation, we are able to occupy our mind. Our mind is occupied by what we are doing, and we are not thinking about what has passed or what is going to happen in the near or distant future. We are thinking about what is happening right at that moment. When our mind is occupied, it does not have room to think about something else. So there is that aspect as well.

Using these techniques helps to bring us to the present and reduces mind's tendency to become scattered and dispersed. We could say that it is a way of harnessing mental energy. When we do breathing meditation and we learn to be in the present, it is like we are trying to gather our mental energy together. When the mind is completely distracted, so much energy is dissipated. It is not the case that we have these distracting thoughts and strong feelings and emotions, and our mental energy level stays intact. It does not. Our mental and emotional activity uses a lot of mental fuel. Worrying, being anxious, getting emotionally upset, or feeling very angry is all very exhausting. The mind is pushed to its limit. The mind is subsequently almost always running on an empty tank. It is no wonder that one may sometimes begin to have a meltdown, as it is commonly referred to.

When we do meditation in this way, we are filling up the tank because we are gathering the mind in. Otherwise, the mind is dispersed and the energy dissipates. This is why meditation is very helpful. It will strengthen the mind. Meditation is a form of mind-training. Mind-training, just like physical training, strengthens the mind. The mind becomes stronger and more resilient so the next time things are difficult, there is less tendency to overreact. This in turn, allows us to see more clearly how we can respond to certain pressing situations in a more insightful and stable way.

In the beginning, this is how we do meditation—not paying too much attention to what is going on in our mind, what is happening, what we are thinking when we are meditating, what we are feeling when we are meditating, or even in terms of what we feel physically. Rather, we are simply focusing on the breath, trying to be in the present, and conserving our mental energy. The only energy spent is in trying to stay with our breath. That is all. This kind of practice, as mentioned before, is explained by the Buddha in the *Anapanasati Sutta*. The Buddha emphasizes this point. After watching the breath come and go, we can also start counting the breath: Exhalation, inhalation, one. Exhalation, inhalation, two... etcetera. This will also help us concentrate.

Mindfulness

The Buddha says that after practicing these breathing techniques for a while, we can drop them. We no longer have to count because our proficiency with the practice has reached a certain level of maturity. Then we can do what is called the "four foundations of mindfulness practice": mindfulness of the body, mindfulness of feeling, mindfulness of mind, and mindfulness of phenomena or the phenomenal world. Here, mindfulness is practiced slightly differently from what was practiced in relation to watching the breath. Here, the point is to become more observant, so that we can actually see what is happening. If we watch the body, we become more aware of our body. We pay attention to our body. This is called "mindfulness of the body."

When we pay more attention to the body we will see that it is made up of many different elements. We tend to reify the concept of body: there is just the body. According to the Buddha, the body has many different parts and elements. It has the vital organs, bodily liquids, pus, blood, flesh, bone, skin, and so on. These are used as objects of contemplation on the body.

The point of this kind of contemplation is that we see how the different parts of the body interact with each other, support each other, complement each other, and also sometimes come into conflict with each other. The Buddha says when we look at the body in that way, we will begin to see that it is a dynamic entity. It is neither static, nor inert. We may think of the physical as something like dead matter but as the Buddha has stated, our body is in a dynamic state all the time. The more we become observant and sensitive to our body, the more we will become aware of its dynamic processes that we were not aware of before.

According to the Buddha, this is an amazing insight. Mindfulness practice done in this way can lead to insight. The insight that the Buddha wants to show us is that all phenomena lack enduring essence. There is no such thing as "body-ness," essence of physicality, or essence of the body. To use a crude example, the body is like a clock and has many different parts. All the different parts have to be working in harmony; otherwise, the clock stops working. If we try to find the essence of the clock, it does not exist.

Similarly, according to the Buddha, to see the insubstantial nature of the body, leads to us seeing the insubstantial nature of all phenomena and the impermanent nature of everything and this is a very important insight. He felt that many of us are driven to find some hidden essence in physical and mental phenomena and, in the process, forget about the importance of that which surrounds us on a daily basis, as if it were not real. We may think, "I have to find the substantial, permanent, hidden essence of all things," but Buddha said that this is a mistaken way to go about it. The Buddha instructed us to practice meditation on the body in this way and similarly when contemplating feelings.[8] "Feelings," in this context, reference sensations such as physical pain. Feelings can be independent of emotions or accompany emotions. They can also be included in mental phenomena.

When we look at feelings, the Buddha said, we can see that they are also in a dynamic state. The Buddha talked about three different kinds of feelings: positive feelings, negative feelings, and neutral feelings. Even a neutral feeling is a form of feeling; not to feel either pleasure or pain is a third kind of feeling that one can have. Again, as with meditation on the body, we can see how these feelings inform and impact on our lives, and shape our inner mental environment—that is to say, how the various permutations of feelings impact upon our various mental states. The contemplation on the impermanent nature of feelings helps us gain more insight into ourselves.

Buddha spoke of mindfulness as not only about us learning to be in the present, but as leading to an understanding of the human condition and the nature of reality. It is not just that we can be in the present and be more attentive and mindful. That is a major part of it but not the most important part. The most important part is to use mindfulness practice to produce this understanding. When mindfulness practice leads to self-understanding, one is maximizing the benefit. The four foundations of mindfulness practice,[9] therefore, leads to understanding, which is a very important outcome.

As laid out by the Buddha in the *Anapanasati Sutta*, this approach of practicing meditation focusing on the self and phenomena is described as a method of "Hinayana" or the first vehicle. In Tibetan Buddhism, after meditating in this way, we often progress to more elaborate practices, some of which are discussed in the following pages.

Overcoming Obstacles in Meditation

As the brothers, Asanga and Vasubandhu,[10] mention in their meditation manual, called *Madhyantavibhanga*, meaning "distinction between center and periphery," (Tib. *uta namje*), the practice of meditation is described in relation to what are called the "five obstacles" and "eight antidotes." So when we do the meditation of tranquility and are trying to be mindful, apart from simply doing meditation, we actually need background information in terms of doing the meditation practice. We have to know what is helpful for meditation and what is not helpful.

The first obstacle to meditation is laziness. At the beginning we may be enthusiastic and really want to practice meditation but, after some time, it is very easy to lose interest or become discouraged. This is especially so if we think we have had no positive signs regarding our meditation practice. For example, we may think that after weeks of meditation, we should start seeing an indication that our meditation is working well.

We may also have the opposite experience. When we begin meditating, maybe for a very short period of time we may think, "This is calming. This is actually quite good," but that is only because it is based more on our feelings than on what is really happening since we may not be very aware of what is going on in our minds. We may think we are feeling calm but, after a little while, if we persist with our practice, we begin to become more aware of our mental states and may start wondering what is going on. We may think, "I'm not practicing meditation properly. Maybe I'm doing something wrong here." We may be too embarrassed to ask for advice when we have this uncertainty, and then our enthusiasm may start to wane.

Maintaining interest in meditation is very important because if we do not, we may become lazy. In Buddhism, laziness is seen as an insidious affliction that we can all suffer from. It deprives us of all kinds of opportunities, spiritual and material. One hour passes by, another day is gone, another week has passed, another month, another year, and so on. Laziness is no friend to alertness, awareness, or consciousness, but it is friends with unconsciousness. This is why laziness is seen as one of the fundamental obstacles to meditation. We need to deal with it, so we use four different kinds of antidotes.

The first one is conviction. Even if we think we are not making progress or are making hardly any progress with meditation practice, we should give ourselves positive feedback regarding meditation. It is like physical exercise. Sometimes we may start exercising and then find it very difficult. We may look at ourselves in the mirror and see that there is hardly any change and find ourselves thinking, "What's the point of this?" Instead of losing heart, if one thinks about the benefit of physical exercise, the lost opportunity, and the potential harm that we may incur in time, regarding our physical health, this could actually help us keep our interest up and our enthusiasm going.

It is like that with meditation. Before going to work in the morning, if we shower and then meditate but are distracted—that is, for example, we might be thinking about what we have to finish doing that day at work—and then realize that our meditation time is up, we may think, "I wasted half an hour. What is the point?" This is the wrong way to think. The very fact that we meditated is something good, something fantastic! One should be aware that "at least I meditated." The fact that we may have been distracted is secondary. The fundamental point is to meditate. Just like exercising the body we should try to do it regularly. Like exercise, our experience of regular meditation practice—while acknowledging that we have meditated without excessively judging the quality of our attention or mind state—will help us gain the conviction we need. We will have the conviction that it is beneficial to do, that it works, that it is something we have to keep doing, and by doing it, life will improve.

When one starts to think like that, this is called "conviction." Conviction is necessary. If we are half-hearted or double-minded we may think, "Maybe it works, maybe it doesn't. I'll give it a go anyway." This approach never works. This is not the way to approach anything, especially meditation and practices like this.

The second one is called "inclination," which means that we have to read literature about meditation. Reading literature like that is extremely helpful, especially that which is inspiring. If we read meditation literature involving great meditators—how they struggled with their minds, lives, and meditation practices, and how they came through, how they triumphed over obstacles in life, we can become inspired. Our inclination to practice meditation would go up a notch or two. We can read biographies of great meditators in the Tibetan Buddhist, Zen, Theravada Buddhist traditions, and so on. Further, in these stories, the meditators are not portrayed as coming to meditation already accomplished. They come to meditation like the rest of us. They gradually progress and then become great meditators. We can draw inspiration from this and we will also want to meditate. The inclination to meditate will definitely be present.

The next one is called "pliancy of body and mind." This is described as "lightness of body and mind." Normally, we may feel heavy inside. Even when we are not tired or suffering from visible symptoms of illness, we can feel a bit heavy, almost dragging our feet on the ground. The mind is often described as "heavy" or "weighed down." In the Tibetan tradition, "buoyancy of the mind" is spoken about quite a lot. Mind should not be like a rock. It is said that mind should be like a ball of cotton wool. Cotton wool bounces around; it is not heavy.

With regard to the body, pliancy comes from diet, exercise, and massage. Again, it depends on how we are feeling. Sometimes we need massage—we do not need more vigorous physical exercise. Sometimes we do not need massage—we need vigorous physical exercise. Pliancy of the body comes from that, and also from *pranayama*, meaning "breathing exercises."

With regard to the mind, pliancy has to come from meditation—doing meditation in a very creative way, not getting bogged down excessively. One is not using the methods of meditation as the end, but seeing the methods only as methods for the mind to develop. Sometimes we get bogged down by being too fixated on the method and, in the process, the crucial point of meditation may be lost. Therefore, we need to have pliancy of the body and mind. This is how it is recommended we should try to deal with laziness.

The fourth antidote to laziness is vigor (Skt: *virya*), which means we have to feel energized. Often, we can find that our mind is speeding, thoughts are happening at great speed, but physically we feel completely lethargic, given to laziness. We do not feel motivated to do anything. It is very easy to become that way, to lose motivation. It is important to learn to motivate ourselves and enjoy what we do. The virtue of vigor comes from taking delight in what we do. Enjoying what we do gives us the kind of energy that we require. This will pick us up and, using that energy, we can forge ahead, we can move beyond our normal deluded mental states such as our indulgence in negative self-talk, which basically reinforces that idea of apathy.

The next obstacle is forgetfulness. Forgetfulness comes from not paying attention, which happens almost all the time for us. We find it very hard to stay focused. This does not mean that if we are meditating, we should be mindful and aware all the time. Rather, it means that we should *try* to be mindful and aware as much as possible. Mindfulness is used as an antidote to forgetfulness; it is not just about being mindful. Mindfulness is also about remembrance. Remembering not to forget is a key part of mindfulness practice; this is why mindfulness is used as an antidote to forgetfulness. Forgetfulness here, as I said, comes from not paying attention or not taking our experiences in. Of course, we take in that which we should not be taking in, but even then we are not really aware of what is going on. Forgetfulness has to be tackled with the use of mindfulness.

Drowsiness and agitation are the next obstacles that one has to overcome. In fact, drowsiness and agitation alternate. Those of us who have been meditating for some time would be very familiar with both of them. When we meditate, either our mind becomes very dull and so we become drowsy, or our mind is completely restless. We go from one to the other.

The antidote to this is awareness. The point is to become aware of these two different states. This is more important than trying not to be drowsy or trying not to be agitated. One recognizes that one is in an agitated state, or that one is feeling drowsy, or that the mind is not very clear or sharp. Awareness has to be applied in that way. If awareness is applied properly, if one is aware, drowsiness and agitation will subside quite naturally. There are instances where as soon as one becomes aware of doing something that one really should not be doing, one cannot continue doing it. If real awareness sets in, it is very hard to continue with that particular type of action.

The fourth obstacle is the obstacle of non-application, which means "not applying the antidotes": the antidote for laziness, the antidote for forgetfulness, and the antidotes for depression and elation, or drowsiness and agitation.

The fifth obstacle is over-application. Sometimes we may get too militaristic in our approach to meditation so we may use the antidotes as weapons to teach the obstacles a lesson! We may use the antidotes even when it is not necessary, just in case. This, again, is not a wise thing to do. Meditation is taught in this way in Mahayana Buddhism,[11] as found in Vasubandhu's meditation manual called *Distinguishing the Middle from the Extremes*.[12]

Esoteric Meditation

When we go into the esoteric practices of Buddhist meditation, we visualize gods and goddesses.[13] We also use our body as an object of meditation, both in motion and in stillness. It is a kind of dynamic interplay between the two. When we do tantric yogic exercises, we are not just doing the yoga, but there are visualizations, meditations that go with the movement. When we are doing meditation in stillness, sitting cross-legged, for example, it involves visualizations, and so on. Then there is dynamism because we still have to relate to what is known in Buddhist esotericism as the "subtle body," in relation to subtle body, in relation to subtle breath (Skt. *prana*), and in relation to subtle energy pathways (Skt. *nadi*). Even though outwardly we are sitting still, inwardly we are in a constant state of movement, dynamic movement. When we do yogic exercises, outwardly we are moving, but inwardly, because we are visualizing, we are still. Outwardly moving and inwardly still, in one case and, in the other case, outwardly still and inwardly moving. Robert Thurman called this "tantric technology."

We do it like that. Again, the traditional part of mindfulness practice is there: mindfulness, awareness, and insight. First, we use the body, breath, mind, and visualization in order to stabilize our mind and put ourselves in a mindful state. Then, at the same time, we realize what our body is like, in essence. Our body, in essence, is non-substantial. As it is said in Buddhist Tantrism or Esotericism: it appears, but is empty of essence. Appearance and emptiness, bliss and emptiness, luminosity and emptiness—this is the tantric vocabulary for the experiences one is able to gain, through engaging in practices like these.

From there, we can go into practices such as *Mahamudra* and *Dzogchen* or *Maha Ati*. The continuity is there in terms of stabilization of the mind with mindfulness and awareness and so on, but how the techniques are applied and used is different. Nevertheless, they are just different versions of the practices that the Buddha himself introduced.

Integral Meditation

Integral Buddhism means that even when it comes to meditation, different kinds of meditation practices can be brought together. We can practice all of them and not think we have to choose one to the exclusion of the others. Depending on what stage we are at and what our needs are, we have to use what we gain most benefit from. This is the key point. Therefore, from the beginning, in the practices of mindfulness such as are to be found in the *Anapanasati Sutta*, to meditation practices as we find them in the Mahamudra and Dzogchen teachings, there is a theme, an underlying thread that strings all these different practices together, that runs through them all. They are not completely unrelated to each other. If we look at other forms of practice apart from meditation, again, we will find this to be the case.

3

Integral Buddhism, Ignorance, and Suffering

Many things have changed in human history but nothing has changed insofar as the way people suffer. That is still the same. Many of us do not have to chop wood to make fire but can just, in a semi-sleepy state, in a zombie-like fashion, wander into our kitchen, turn on our stove, and cook something. This has not reduced suffering. If we compare how much people suffer in the more advanced countries with how people suffer in undeveloped countries and developing countries, there is hardly a difference in terms of psychological suffering. In terms of physical pain, there is a big difference but, by and large, in terms of suffering, there is little difference.[14]

This is fundamentally what drew the Buddha to search for meaning in life 2,500 years ago. Seeing suffering around him prompted him to look for a solution to what he was observing. The Buddha was not thinking, "Why am I here? Who created me?" Rather, he saw suffering around him and, as it is said, he saw death, he saw sickness, and he saw old age. He saw people suffering and it made him think. He realized even though he was young at the time that "I, too, will be like these people. I will get old, I will get sick, and I am going to die." He thought, "I have to find some solution to these kinds of experiences."

After years of searching for the solution to suffering, the Buddha realized that the cause of suffering was our lack of self-knowledge and self-understanding. This ignorant state perpetuates much of the suffering we experience. Further, we are susceptible to repeating the mistakes that cause us suffering, like a person addicted to gambling who does not realize that the nature of gambling is skewed towards loss, and so they repeat destructive patterns. In our ignorance, we do the same. The Buddha called this "samsara" or "cyclic existence." Due to views and perspectives that come from ignorance, our world is governed by unruly and conflicting emotions.[15] When our mind is disturbed with emotional excesses such as excessive greed, lust, anger, resentment, bitterness, and confusion, we do not think clearly. The level of suffering that we experience is then exacerbated.

The personalized world that we construct for ourselves, from a Buddhist perspective, is seen as a prison. This is what is meant by "samsara." Samsara is not the world that we live in. We are enveloped. The world itself, taken as a whole, is not samsara. Samsara is that personal world, full of illusion and delusion, which we have constructed for ourselves and, because of this, we do not see clearly. Therefore, the personalized world created with our samsaric mind is deceptive, yet we take it to be real. We take it to be the truth. This is what Buddhism means when referring to "our state of ignorance."

Ignorance, in Buddhism, is understood in many different ways, according to different schools of thought. Fundamentally speaking, all Buddhist traditions agree on one point, which is that there are two different types of ignorance. One is innate ignorance. That is, we are born with ignorance. The other is what one might call "acquired ignorance," which comes from the accumulation of experiences and our personalized response to those experiences. It comes from learning to see things in the wrong way. The innate form of ignorance has to do with some notion, some understanding that there is something called "me and mine," as Buddhism says, some innate tendency to cling onto the concept of a permanent self. Without having thought about it, without being tutored into thinking about an immutable soul, having had none of these religious or philosophical instructions, automatically, just instinctively, we think that there is something called "me and mine" or "I and other." This "I" or "me" is seen as something abiding, something fixed. That is, we think, "I have my feelings, I have my memories, I believe I am these." However, from a Buddhist perspective, we are none of these.

The reason this samsaric state is called "ignorance" is because it prevents us from seeing how things truly are. Due to our grasping at and fixating on our false self, we extrapolate this false self onto the world, others, and everything else. One begins to cling onto self and other as being unchanging, solid, stable, fixed, and objectively existing. Instinctively, in a very defensive fashion, we think there is something called "me" hidden inside us, trapped within the body, and that there is something called "other" out there—again, existing in a very fixed way. To see "oneself" and to see "other" in that way, or to see "myself" and the duality of "me and mine" in that way, as described in the Buddhist teachings, is a distortion—we do not see things clearly. We fail to see things from the right perspective. According to Buddhism, ignorance means simply that: not being able to see things from the correct perspective. What we perceive is off-key, distorted, and that distortion comes from thinking something is intractable, immutable, and fixed. From the Buddhist perspective, there is no fixity and there is nothing immutable. We mistakenly conceptualize about things in terms of essences, substances, rather than in relation to conditions, processes, and becoming. Seeing in this fashion is not innocuous. It is not some harmless state of not knowing, some innocent state of not knowing. Far from being innocent, this lack of knowledge brings about consequences that are harmful to our relationship with oneself, others, and the world.

This is why an integral approach to Buddhism is so important. The answer to ignorance is to build insight, understanding, and knowledge about the nature of existence and our lives. The more knowledge we have about how we perpetuate samsara, the more power we have to overcome and transform it. We have more power over our unruly emotions, or to use Carl Jung's notion, the shadow aspect of ourselves.[16]

In Buddhism, learning about all aspects of oneself is the key to bringing knowledge into our lives. It is not sufficient just to learn about the Buddhist practice of meditation, or to learn a little about Buddhist psychology, or Buddhist philosophy, or healing, or arts, such as painting, singing, and dancing. In Tibet, for example, there is a rich tradition of philosophy, psychology, and the many art forms. In the West, followers of Tibetan Buddhism may not wish to embrace the many aspects of this tradition, as they see them as being culturally determined. This does not mean that these cannot then be translated into a corresponding Western form of dance, music, or art and crafts. It is not said that Western forms of singing and dancing cannot be incorporated into the Buddhist tradition. When Buddhism was introduced to Tibet, for example, the Tibetans retained the essence and purity of the religion, while intertwining Buddhist principles into their cultural mores and customs. Thus, it can be embraced in such a way in the West. The fundamental point is that Buddhism says all these are important to bring insight and knowledge into our lives. They are all necessary.

If we choose to seriously embrace Buddhism, this does not mean that we have to be experts in all areas. We may choose to be more learned in one field, such as Buddhist philosophy, but the idea is that we should try to learn at least a little about the range of disciplines within the tradition. If one has some interest in doing meditation, one should not exclude activities like studying the texts or learning philosophy and the art forms. Practitioners do not need to restrict themselves in that way. If there is some interest in learning psychology, one does not simply focus on that and not think about physical well-being and physical health.

Self and Personhood

Not everything we experience originates from mental problems or mental distress. Sometimes our mental distress may have a physiological basis. For example, we may not be feeling good physically, but we are also feeling tired, depressed, and generally down. We may be down because we are feeling weak and generally lacking strength. So the physical experience begins to be felt mentally.

We have to address all these aspects of ourselves. It is almost a cliché to say this but one needs to take something of a holistic approach. One looks at oneself as a whole person. This really goes hand in hand with the Buddhist idea of "the person" because in Buddhism, understanding "the person" or our personhood is the most important thing. There is not the idea of some kind of self. "Self" is literally a constructed idea that we have in terms of our identity, but the person, on the other hand, has many dimensions, many aspects, and there are many different levels of being that one can talk about, in terms of shallowness and depth. If we think about self, then the self is an abstract idea. We abstract this notion of the self from different aspects of ourselves, and then objectify that notion and make it into a thing or entity. It is basically made up. That is the Buddhist view.

When we try to attend to the needs of our own selfhood, according to Buddhism, we have embarked on a self-defeating exercise because there is no self to be fixed. You might think, "Oh, I'm such a loser." I am sure many of us have had those thoughts at times. Following these kinds of thoughts we may think, "I'm that kind of person," and in this context it means, "I am that kind of person who has that notion of self who thinks of themselves as being that kind of being or person." Then it is abstracted. It is abstracted from the person's diverse emotional range, in terms of physical embodiment, and in terms of that individual's intellectual endowment.

In Buddhism, through study and meditation, we build an understanding of how suffering arises and how we perpetuate it through misguided ideas about ourselves. When we understand how we have created our personal suffering, we are in a better position to begin to overcome it. We can see that to put an end to it, we have to let go of clinging onto some idea of the self as a self-existing entity and focus more on the person, the individual, because as a person we cannot remain stuck. A person does not get stuck. It is not possible. A person thinks they are stuck when they become fixated on a fabricated notion of self. They have ideas relating to arrested self-development, thinking, "I'm not going anywhere, nothing is happening to me, nothing is going right in my life." Thinking negatively in a fixated and fabricated manner is exactly what is not serving us well. This is what reinforces the idea of the self and, as a result, our personhood becomes neglected. We end up neglecting ourselves because we are so caught up in this illusory idea of, "What is the real me?" We are always in search of that. We can spend our whole life trying to find out.

Buddha's view was that this pursuit is a useless exercise because, often, it will depend on our mood. When we are feeling optimistic and good, we think the "real me" is fantastic, all-powerful, omnipotent, and omni-benevolent. When we are not feeling so good, we think we are the worst of the worst; we cannot think of anybody worse than us. We believe that this is the "real me." When we go through this kind of polarity, one moment our ego is inflated and we think we are the greatest, and the next moment the ego deflates like a balloon, all that puff has gone, and we have shrunk.

We may think in that fashion, but nothing of this is true. This is the Buddhist view. In that way an illusion is created about ourselves. Whenever we think, "I have to find my real self" we go through this and it is very time-consuming, emotionally taxing, and very costly. As Buddhists say, we become completely self-obsessed.

If we can just put the obsession of looking for the "real me" aside, even for a very short time, and look at ourselves as a multi-dimensional person, and then start addressing all aspects of ourselves, we will be in a much better position to understand how we inflict suffering upon ourselves. We begin to address those issues and we see tangible results in a short period of time. If we start to think in a philosophical manner, clarify and organize our thoughts and psychological experiences, deal with our emotions and feelings,[17] and look into our physical dimension and needs, we are effectively addressing ourselves as a whole person.

When attempting to clarify our thoughts, we are likely to become mono-focal. For example, we may zoom in on an idea such as wanting to be slim and believing all our troubles will then disappear if that happens. Alternatively, we may believe problems will subside if we become highly emotionally developed and thus people will feel connected to us. We may think that by doing so, we will never be lonely. We may want to be smart, get a degree or a doctorate in philosophy, studying all the great Eastern and Western philosophers. We think, "If I cultivate my intellect, I can win every argument. When I have an argument with somebody about any topic, if I can silence that person and show how smart I am, then I will be somebody. Then I will be great." We become mono-focal again and again.

This mono-focal thinking reinforces our notion of selfhood—that false sense of self based on mono-focal self-obsession—instead of personhood, the totality of our inclusive, multi-dimensional human condition. Reinforcing our notion of selfhood limits us because so many other aspects of us are neglected. This is because of our tendency to be obsessed with one aspect of our experience at the expense of the other aspects that we should also be pursuing. We have many needs as human beings and these should be attended to. We cannot attend to all of them at the same level, with the same intensity, or with the same devotion, but none of them should be completely neglected. Of course, we have limited time in our lives so we need to pursue or focus on some things more than others. For example, even if we do not want the body of a bodybuilder, doing some exercise and trying to eat properly is very important. In Buddhism, this is also seen as a form of mindfulness practice. It is like mindfulness in action, like the mindfulness of walking and of eating. Zen Buddhists and many other traditions are in accord with that.

Four noble truths, Ethics, and the Integral approach
The four noble truths are listed as follows:
1. The noble truth of suffering
2. The noble truth of the origin of suffering
3. The noble truth of the cessation of suffering
4. The noble truth of the way or path leading to the cessation of suffering

In Buddhism, our starting point is the four noble truths. The four noble truths have to do with recognizing that suffering exists, and then looking for the cause of suffering. Having found the cause of suffering, it is then about gaining the knowledge that suffering can cease, that we can put an end to it, and that there is a path we can follow to achieve this end, this goal. This is why we practice Buddhism. According to Buddhism, this is the only reason. It is not because we are trying to find out who created us and why we are here on this planet and not somewhere else, or who is responsible, apart from our parents, for our being here. Nor is it anything to do with who created our parents and our parents' parents. We are not looking at it like that but rather, we are looking at it in a practical way and seeing where we are situated.

The way to the cessation of suffering, the fourth noble truth, is related to paying attention to all aspects of our person. We should spend time in meditation, study, and pay attention to the ethical dimension of our conduct, how we interact with others, and relate to the world. We should also pay attention to them because, in Buddhism, ethics and aesthetics are seen as being closely related—for example, an ethically edifying action, and beauty are linked. Ethics and morality, even in the West, are sometimes seen as something quite different from each other. Morality is about rules that ask, "Which are the morally right and wrong actions to take? How can we clearly define the particulars of right and wrong?" This concept does exist in Buddhism, however moral rules are seen as inferior to an ethical approach. In Buddhism, we endeavor to rise above moral codes so that we can learn to be ethical—that is, we consider what is ethically appropriate, in relation to the situations and circumstances in which we find ourselves at any given time. To be ethical is also about "good" and "bad"; however, rather than being moralistic, "good" is defined as that which is wholesome and life-enhancing, and "bad" is understood as that which is life-destroying. This is used as the criterion for whether one is behaving in an ethical fashion or not. If what one is doing is life-enhancing, that is good. If it is life-destroying, even if morally compliant, it may not be good from an ethical standpoint.

In Buddhism, therefore, finding the way out of suffering has to be based on this sense of ethical awareness: awareness of one's environment, awareness of others' desires, needs, and aspirations, and pursuing one's own interests, desires, aspirations, in parallel to the desires, aspirations, and needs of others. We can subsequently work with people more effectively, considerately, intelligently, and compassionately, rather than thinking of others either as people who can help us get ahead or people who will create obstacles in our path. We thus avoid measuring people solely in relation to their ability to help us move forward or what we perceive as their intention to create obstacles for us.

Just being ethical is not enough, however. From a Buddhist perspective, as mentioned earlier, one should also practice meditation, study Buddhist philosophy, psychology, and learn about physical awareness. By doing so, one learns to be more skillful. Through understanding the human condition better, we can work with others more effectively. The idea is that if we have this approach, even if people may want to put obstacles in our path, their power is, in a sense, disabled. So often, by reacting to someone's negativity in a negative fashion we actually further empower the other person; we are helping that person to have power over us. We can end up thinking about them all the time. While we are eating, while we are sleeping, while we are working, we find ourselves obsessively thinking about them—even our food does not taste good. Thoughts of that person can take over our lives and our world can become colored by such negativity.

In Buddhism, we should try to bring all of our person into our practice and understand that how we live our life is fundamental. Personally, I find it exciting to study and compare Western psychology and Buddhist psychology, and also Western philosophy and Buddhist philosophy, because this is helpful in terms of how we live our lives. It, however, will only be helpful if it makes a difference to how we live. If there is no change in how we live, then we are not really practicing Buddhism properly. We could be meditating every day, but if we are not really changing how we live our lives, how we interact with others, and what we do with our lives, our effort is going to waste. Even very devoted Buddhist practitioners can become mono-focal with regard to their Buddhist practice. Therefore, it is important that even if we may emphasize a particular aspect of Buddhist practice, we should not exclude and neglect the other aspects.

Ethics

In Buddhism, the ethical dimension is called "the feet of our spiritual practice." Accordingly, ethics should carry us as we walk through life. Ethics can allow our lives to work well because an ethical approach carries our other pursuits. As I mentioned, ethics and aesthetics are related. Shantideva[18] and other Mahayana teachers have said that even our physical appearance has a close relationship with ethics. They say that you could be the most physically beautiful person, but if you have uncontrollable rage, you will be ugly.

If we can learn to understand our emotions, then without suppressing them or pretending we do not have pleasant or unpleasant emotions, we learn to take all our experiences on board and work with them. Then we do not have to express them in a negative way. So staying with, observing, and working with our negative emotions as they arise, encourages an attitude of accommodation, as opposed to suppression or excessive aversion, or the tendency to bury or disown a negative emotion. This approach can overcome the somewhat unconscious "festering" of negativity. Failure to accommodate a negative emotion can cause it to reemerge in other negative ways so giving negativity air and owning and addressing it, without fuelling it, is an ethical way to improve the quality of our lives.

In Mahayana Buddhism, it is said that the reason ethics and aesthetics go together very well is because physical expressions reflect what is going on in our mind. If a person is at ease with their emotions, then that will be projected and will be aesthetically pleasant. If they have not come to terms with their emotions, then even if they do not show emotions, there can be other indicators.

There may be a certain manner, a posture, a grimace, a frown, and aspects of their lifestyle may indicate disturbances, such as eating too much or not eating enough, sleeping all the time or not sleeping, and so on.

This is why in Buddhism it is said that totally integrated people have a sense of ease in themselves and that is beautiful. If they are at ease, then that person is beautiful. If one is not at ease but self-divided, fighting within oneself then that comes through. When we are self-divided, we can have problems getting on with others. If one is fighting with oneself, one will fight with others. Therefore, pursuit of the Dharma in every respect is seen as a way to bring wisdom and knowledge into our lives so that we become less self-divided, wisdom being the last of the three principles of Buddhism, mentioned earlier, of which conduct and meditation are the first two. This will help us to deal with daily situations. As Buddhism says, "We have to understand our human condition—why we suffer and how we suffer." This is the starting point.

4
The Integral Approach to Overcoming Suffering

Buddhism does not say "life is suffering," as some people think. Rather, Buddhism says, "How we conduct ourselves and how we see the world, how we interact with others, causes suffering." This is why some of us suffer more than others. Even when two people live in the same environment, one could be suffering more than the other. How do we best deal with suffering? Contrary to what some people think, it is not said that in order to overcome suffering we have to try to become enlightened. Buddhism says that we have to deal with our pain and suffering in a practical way. It does not say that gaining enlightenment is the only answer. It is the answer, in one sense, but that is the distant goal. In Buddhism, we are instructed to set two different goals: one is the distant goal of attaining enlightenment, nirvana, and the other is the more immediate goal of reducing pain and suffering in our immediate future. It is not the case that we have to wait until we die or attain enlightenment to be free of all manner of pain and suffering. We do not have to wait to be happy.

Buddhism says that although there is an interrelationship between pain and suffering, we still have to distinguish between pain and suffering. Of course, sometimes pain and suffering go together, but at other times they do not. Some painful things may be unavoidable and other painful things may actually be good for us. Pain has an unavoidable aspect; thus managing pain with a healthy attitude can produce very good results. Suffering of any kind is not good for us. Suffering imposes excessive conceptualization on an experience we see as negative, thus exaggerating the circumstances. It does not produce benefit for anyone, whereas even though at the time they may be unpleasant, certain profound, painful, and upsetting experiences could be beneficial. They may actually go towards us developing skills to cope better with life so that one begins to suffer less. By learning to deal with painful things, one learns how to reduce suffering.

For example, in terms of Buddhist practice, we need to learn to overcome suffering, but some element of physical hardship could, in fact, be good. It is good training, both physically and mentally. We can become very soft and vulnerable to any small irritation; we cannot bear it. It is character-building to engage in rigorous physical practice of different kinds, including mild ascetic practices, being in the wilderness, spending a certain period of time in solitude, without heating and the modern comforts, roughing it and so on. We become more courageous, more daring. We learn not to shun any little difficulties or obstacles that we may experience. We become more adventurous and therefore no longer shy away from taking a certain element of risk.

Some people living in comfort and not really in significant pain are suffering. In that sense, I suppose they have some kind of pain, but their suffering is avoidable. Pain and suffering are different things and yet sometimes we may think that when Buddhism talks about suffering, it means all kinds of painful experiences, and that to overcome suffering, we then have to overcome all those painful experiences.

It is important to first consider how to separate pain and suffering. With suffering, we may be able to distinguish between the type of suffering we cannot overcome until we advance on the spiritual path, and the type of suffering that we can actually avoid.

Our immediate goal then is not to get rid of all painful experiences and all suffering, but to pick up the skills to help us deal with the painful experiences and suffering that we may experience. The classic example of suffering that we are not able to avoid is old age. Getting old is going to happen for most of us. We cannot put it off. We cannot say, "I'm not ready to get old yet." It does not matter what we think, we are going to get old anyway. This can produce suffering. Sickness is another example that Buddhism speaks about. When we get sick, we suffer, and that is something that we have to deal with; then there is death, of course—facing our own mortality.

To reiterate, there is suffering that we cannot avoid which we have to learn to deal with. Other forms of suffering that we experience are actually avoidable because they are brought on by disturbances in our mind. By learning and picking up the skills that will allow us to see how this is happening, we can lead a more satisfying and wholesome life. We will also be leading a spiritual life if we do it like that. In that way, all the practices that we do in Buddhism are about reducing suffering by trying to understand ourselves better.

Misunderstanding and Excessive Mental Reflection

Much of the suffering that we experience is brought on by too much reflection on our experiences. In other words, thinking too much about our experiences causes more confusion in the mind. Trying to look deeply into the mind in search of a definitive meaning can be disturbing. How we interpret experiences is often predetermined by our opinions, habitual patterns, and ways of thinking. For example, a partner, friend, or family member may be feeling ill and become quiet and unresponsive, and we may misunderstand and interpret their silence as anger or moodiness. Further, we may think about the other times when our partner has been unresponsive and become angry ourselves, leading to disharmony or confusion. The whole incident is simply a misunderstanding. In other words, we have conceptualized excessively on our experience and it has caused us suffering. We have personalized the incident and experienced hurt and dissatisfaction, which has then caused more confusion. With more confusion come disturbances within us, and between ourselves and others. Due to such conceptual complexity, we can become more disturbed because we cannot see our way out. It becomes overwhelming. This is the irony of the Buddhist practices. On the one hand, Buddhism teaches us to look into ourselves so that we have greater understanding, more self-knowledge. On the other hand, a lot of our problems are produced by thinking too much about our experiences and when we do that, we get a distorted version of whatever it is that we think has happened. Whatever we think has happened is either not going on or, if it is going on, is not happening in the way we think it is. Even so, a distinction may be made between a Buddhist practitioner authentically looking within during spiritual practice—working with confusion and gaining self-knowledge—and someone looking within in a fixated, attached, and self-obsessed fashion and thus creating more confusion.

In any case, Buddhism says we have very deep-seated, entrenched habits regarding how we see and experience things. Fundamentally, Buddhism teaches us not to take everything that we experience at face value. This is the opposite of what many people think Buddhism says. There is a mistaken belief that Buddhism is about our own experiences and, if we experience something, then it is true. Actually, Buddhism says completely the opposite. Buddhism says that because we think it is true, we should actually be a little more skeptical about what it is we are experiencing and not think, "This must be true because I experienced it." Just because we experience something, does not mean it is real. Of course, it is real insofar as we experienced it, but it is more like what happens when we have a dream. When we have been dreaming and we wake up, we know that we have dreamt it. Of course, to the extent that we had a dream, it is real, but nothing about the dream is real. Similarly, because we have had certain experiences does not mean we should take them too seriously, as being completely true, because the experience depends on our habitual tendencies, our demeanor, and our attitude at the time. This is very important because it goes hand in hand with the Buddhist notion of letting go.

As many Buddhist masters have said, we experience things very intensely because we take what we experience to be real. We take everything so seriously. Because we take it all so seriously and our experiences are intense, we therefore become agitated and our emotions and feelings[19] become exaggerated and flare up. This happens because, as Buddhism says, we have the ingrained instincts of a self-protective response. Everything that we experience, we think of in terms of how to protect ourselves, how to keep anything that we see as threatening to our well-being and sense of selfhood, at bay. However, Buddhism says that we do not have to keep certain experiences at bay because what is really troubling, the source of our troubles, is inside. It actually lies in how we view ourselves. In other words, whoever we think is harmed when we have a disturbing experience instinctively thinks that this unpleasant experience has been harmful to "me."

According to Buddhism, we are mistaken on many different levels. Firstly, the source of harm, if such harm has been caused, is not really external. Secondly, the harm that we think has been created is, in itself, in its reality, contingent on the belief of the individual. The more we believe in the harm that was caused, the greater the intensity of the experience will be. The less we believe it, the less harm will be caused. The ego or the self that we think is being damaged or harmed in some way, in itself, is not actually something that can be harmed in the true sense of the word, as we would normally understand it. What does this mean then? It means that our experiences are "really real" only to the extent that we think they are. The degree of reality is not objectively established. It is contingent on the subject, on the state of the individual concerned. It is precisely because of this that Dharma can be helpful and useful. This is why we can actually use Dharma to deal with life's difficulties.

The Buddhist view is that if it were not so, that our experiences are contingent, any damage done to one's sense of selfhood would be lethal. It would go right through to one's being. However, Buddhism says this is not the case. In addition, if life experiences were not contingent on the individual subjective states of the individual concerned, then whatever we experienced would be real, and whatever was real, immutable, entirely certain, and solid, would thus be harder to overcome. Something that is real on the relative level, to put it in Buddhist terms, can be overcome.[20] Yes, suffering exists, but suffering exists only on the relative level. It is precisely for these reasons that if we pick up different Buddhist practices, we will be able to reduce our level of suffering.

Pursuing an Integral Approach

Therefore, we need to pursue Buddhadharma—which is another name for Dharma, the Buddhist teachings—but we do not have to think of Buddhadharma purely in terms of studying the teachings or doing meditation. Buddhism says we have to address the three aspects of our being: body, our vocal aspect or speech, and mind. We can do different kinds of practices to deal with these three aspects of one's being. With the body, we do yoga and learn to do ritualized gestures within the tantric practices. These are practiced in order to integrate the body into one's spiritual practice. Other physical practices are mentioned in terms of the body, for example, dancing. With regard to the speech aspect, practices such as chanting, singing, and pranayama are mentioned.[21] With the mind, we do different kinds of meditational practice, including tranquility meditation where we watch the breath, and contemplation, visualization, and analysis. Such meditational practices help us understand the mind and how our mental processes and thoughts affect us. We also use visualization to uplift, purify, and awaken the mind. We can do all these different kinds of practices and think of them as part of Dharma practice.

So Dharma practice is not just about working with the mind, but involves all aspects of us. In Buddhism, when we talk about self-transformation, it is not seen as purely mental. Self-transformation is seen as transformation of the totality of one's being. One's physical body, one's vocal capacity, and one's mind all become transformed simultaneously. In Mahayana Buddhism, for example, we call this "attaining vajra body, vajra speech, and vajra mind." The expression "vajra body, vajra mind," means "indestructible body, indestructible mind."

The transformation that we strive for is not purely a spiritual journey. In the West when we use the word "spirituality," it has the connotation of contrasting with the corporeal: you have the corporeal aspect and then the spiritual aspect. However, in Buddhism, there is no tradition of seeing body and mind, corporeality and spirituality, in dualistic terms. You could say you have a spiritualized corporeality and a "corporealized" spirituality. For example, the highest aspect, the most profound aspect of buddha's body is called "dharmakaya," which corresponds to buddha's spiritual aspect, but it is still called kaya, meaning "body." It is like the embodiment of buddha's spiritual attainment. What is corporeal also becomes spiritualized through karmic purification. In Buddhism, karmic imprints and tendencies are spoken about. These do not operate purely on a mental level. We have physical karmic imprints and tendencies, so when we engage in Dharma practice, we are not only freeing ourselves from the mental karmic imprints and tendencies, but we are also freeing ourselves from the physical karmic imprints and tendencies.[22] Our body stores its own version of memory. Freeing the body of this is a way of transforming one's body. Doing different practices that deal with the body frees it up; the body is then reconditioned and is not subsequently bound by these physical karmic imprints and tendencies.

In this way, Dharma is used on three different levels. If we are conditioned in a restrictive way, it can be said that we have conditioned ourselves in a negative way. As we create much of our suffering, we need to recondition ourselves. "Reconditioning" means adopting different ways of behaving, thinking, perceiving things, and interacting with others and then going beyond that so that one can operate in a spontaneous fashion, which in Buddhist terms means that we then do not create fresh karma. This reconditioning has to happen on the physical as well as the mental level. The mental aspect is very important and this is why Buddhism puts more emphasis on the mind but, nevertheless, the physical aspect is not to be ignored. It is important to develop an understanding of how one can incorporate different kinds of Buddhist practices to make one's life much more fulfilling and constructive, and thus reduce suffering.

Buddhism says that if we are suffering too much, not only are we deprived of the opportunity to live a satisfying and fulfilling life, but we also deprive ourselves of the opportunity to really connect with others and the world. From a Buddhist point of view, this should be seen as extremely important when it comes to attaining our full potential. According to Buddhism, we cannot reach our full potential as a human being until we have learned to connect with others. If we are living with extended and excessive periods of misery and suffering, it is hard not to be deeply concerned about oneself. This can lead to a type of self-obsession where it is difficult to concern ourselves about anybody else or, indeed, have concerns regarding the world.

For this reason, it is important not to think of Buddhism as a teaching to help us resign ourselves to a life that has already gone to the dogs. It is easy to think that Buddhism teaches that life is illusory and has no meaning and, for example, from a cynical and nihilistic perspective, think, "Why get married because it might end in divorce? Why make money when I could end up broke? Why enjoy being pampered, because one day I may become sick? Why do anything, because it is all empty?" Believing that everything is illusory and so therefore has no meaning is a misinterpretation of what Buddhism is really saying.

Rather, Buddhism is saying that many fortunate and unfortunate events can happen but, in the light of all these possibilities, we should make the most of life. If we have a completely unrealistic view of life, we are setting ourselves up for disappointment and frustration, which will only compound our mental suffering. While knowing that all these things can happen, it is sensible to try to make a good life for ourselves. Recognizing that things are not enduring and that there is an insubstantial quality to life, should give us motivation to enjoy and participate and be fully connected with our loved ones, experiences, and the world. This is because we can see life as precious, whereas a nihilistic view diminishes the richness and beauty in life, simply focusing on the fact that things do not last. A nihilistic view can diminish one's experience because the world is simply not taken seriously and is devalued. When we see how precious life is, it means that we can live a much more satisfying and constructive life. It is not a reason to give up on life. It is a reason to live one's life more fully, based on a more realistic assessment of what life is actually about, with all its ups and downs, joys and pains, successes and failures.

According to Buddhism, if we learn to think like this, we will be much better off. That is, we can avoid extreme views such as nihilism and eternalism and, through being well connected, we can respond to changing circumstances. For example, by moderating our expectations and being more realistic, we can avoid plunging into the darkness of despair even in the most difficult of circumstances. Further, when things are going very well, when we are riding high, we are no longer taking things for granted as we did formerly; we will not lose our ground only to then take a fall. One has a more realistic perspective on life and one builds on that.

It is my hope that by talking about integral Buddhism, it will become clearer that it involves incorporating different aspects of one's life and seeing all of these as part of one's Dharma practice. Diminishing our relationship with the world to avoid suffering is not part of the Buddhist path. This approach can only increase suffering. The Buddhist approach is asking us to embrace life more fully, more realistically, and with passion.

Renunciation

Buddhism emphasizes the importance of relationship—relationship with oneself, with others, and the world—and it should be a well-integrated relationship, encompassing many aspects and dimensions. It is not a requirement that we renounce joy, interest, passion, care, love, and so forth.

If we understand it this way, we can put the Buddhist notion of renunciation and detachment into proper perspective. "Renunciation" does not mean we renounce everything. It means that we can choose to renounce certain things so that we can pursue others more passionately. For example, if someone chose to be a monk or a nun, they would renounce married life to create more time to pursue activities that they are more interested in. It does not mean that they have renounced everything. It is about prioritizing. Monks and nuns have their own interests and passions. What one is giving up for what reason, seems to be the point; "renunciation" does not mean one has given up on life. It is about making a choice in life, saying, "I choose this rather than that. I choose this lifestyle, rather than that lifestyle in order to find fulfillment in my life."

If we think of it like that, we can see the Buddhist idea of renunciation and detachment in the right context, and not in a nihilistic way. Particularly when Buddhism was new in the West, translations of Buddhism often presented the teachings in a way that could be interpreted as nihilistic. It could be read as life-denying, pessimistic, as if somehow life itself was a bad thing, and that we would be better off not being born. This is obviously not the Buddhist view. I wish to emphasize this here.

According to Buddhism, every time we do something that benefits us in a positive way, this is a Dharma practice. Anything we do that is detrimental to our well-being, is non-dharma or non-dharmic. This is why previous masters have often said that sometimes when we do what we think is Dharma practice, and we are doing it with the wrong motivation or incorrectly, we actually do not get dharmic benefit. We may incur some harm because of the distortion introduced into it. Sometimes we may do something not so obviously dharmic, but it is nevertheless dharmic and therefore produces positive results. In that way, whatever we think, whatever we feel, whatever we do—all these have impacted on us as human beings, and so we need to look at all aspects of ourselves, which is an integral approach.

For example, taking an interest in astronomy, doing medicine, art and craft, painting, making music, dramatics—all these can be used as part of dharmic practice. In the Tibetan Buddhist canon, there are texts on all kinds of subject matter. Engaging in logic, trying to think clearly, is also seen as part of Dharma practice and actually as a very important part, because our thinking is normally disorganized. Learning to organize our thoughts is very helpful because it clarifies our mind. Then, when we put our mind to something in terms of contemplation or a similar activity, it is much easier for us to stay with those thoughts and follow them through properly. We can actually see what is going on instead of the mind going everywhere, as normally happens.

Mindfulness, Awareness, and Thinking Clearly

In a later chapter, I will talk about Buddhist psychology in more depth. Briefly, in relation to the integral approach where "thinking logically" is included as part of Dharma practice, since our thoughts, emotions, and feelings go hand in hand with each other, having disorganized thoughts means we will have very confused emotions. If we think more clearly, our emotions will begin to respond accordingly. This is the Buddhist view. Buddhism does not say we should practice mindfulness so that we do not get caught up in our thoughts. Rather, Buddhism says that if we practice mindfulness and awareness, we can learn to organize our thoughts properly. We cannot just be told to organize our thoughts. We need to have a technique and, in Buddhism, we use mindfulness practice for that. First, we use mindfulness practice to learn to gather our mind, and then we use mindfulness to deal with different mental states and processes. These different techniques are designed to give us the skills to reduce the level of suffering we experience, due to our unruly mind.

Fundamentally, mindfulness is applied in a deliberate way, and awareness is a natural state of being that arises from having built up an effective mindfulness practice—in other words, an excellent habitual pattern of observing. Mindfulness is practiced and exercised in order to develop awareness, whereas awareness naturally arises. Mindfulness is applied to our meditation to help us see what is going on with our mind and our mental states. It also allows us to know how we are managing our body and breath, for example, and maintaining an erect spine. Mindfulness is what brings our mind back to the breath or object of meditation when our mind has wandered. The practice of mindfulness requires application, effort, vigor, and remembrance. Awareness is effortless. It is not a practice but rather a state or attainment.

5

Working with Suffering and Becoming Stronger

According to Buddhism, much of the suffering we experience is avoidable. Instead of thinking, "I want a life without suffering and pain," we should be thinking, "How can I make my life more resilient, more satisfying, and less painful, where I have less suffering?" This should be our goal and it is achievable. A life totally without suffering and pain is very difficult to achieve, but we could think, "I can actually do without some of the unnecessary suffering. I can achieve this." We can then pick up the necessary skills to do this. The idea is that a lot of physical pain and suffering is unavoidable but the level of the suffering we do experience could be reduced if we change our attitude towards suffering. If we have a better attitude towards old age, death, sickness, etcetera, we will suffer less. This does not mean we will not suffer at all, but we will suffer less. If we have a non-accommodating attitude, we will suffer more.

In the previous chapter, I spoke about the reason we follow the Dharma, why we practice, and pain and suffering. I said that pain and suffering were different from each other. There are different kinds of pain. Many of them are unavoidable, but there are others that are avoidable. If we look at the teachings on the four noble truths, we can also see this. When we speak about the noble truth of suffering, the noble truth of the cause of suffering, the noble truth of cessation of suffering, and the way out of suffering, the word "noble" does not actually mean that the truth of suffering, for example, is noble because it is true. The "noble" part has to do with the individual practitioner. Someone who tries to understand the truth of suffering, or the truth of the cause of suffering, is a noble person. Someone who actually tries to understand the four noble truths is a noble individual or an *arya*.[23]

The first two truths basically describe our human condition, and with the last two truths, the emphasis is on prescribing what one should do in order to relieve oneself of suffering. So the four noble truths have descriptive and prescriptive components attached to them.

Three Kinds of Suffering

The idea of suffering (Skt. *duhkha*) has a wide connotation. Three kinds of suffering are usually spoken about. The first is called the "suffering of conditioned existence," the second is the "suffering of change," and the third is the "suffering of suffering." The suffering of conditioned existence is similar to existential angst, and is built into our condition. It is therefore hard to avoid. With the second type, known as the "suffering of change," much of it, through practice, we can learn to overcome or deal with more effectively. The third one, the suffering of suffering, in most cases, we can learn to overcome; through training, we need not subject ourselves to exaggerated forms of suffering. We may be suffering already, and we make it worse. For example, if we are struck down with some dreaded illness, then due to improper attitude and unhelpful emotional reactions, this suffering is made worse. It is compounded. Hence, it is called the "suffering of suffering."

The first kind of suffering has to do with conditioned existence itself. Sometimes we say "samsara is suffering," and from that we may conclude that this conditioned existence, this cyclic existence, is *itself* suffering. This is not the case. The suffering comes from the discrepancy or lack of correspondence between how things are and how we think things ought to be. According to Buddhism, the suffering arises from our inability to accept reality. Due to our ignorance, unresolved emotional issues, and attachments, we do not actually deal properly with events as they unfold. Therefore we suffer. We think everything ought to be different from how it actually is and because of this, we do not see conditioned existence itself for what it is. We see conditioned existence as being something different.

Craving and Desire

Due to this, suffering ensues. The cause of suffering, which in Buddhism is called "craving," is like an accentuated form of desire. Often it is said in English translations of Buddhist terms that the cause of suffering is desire. While "desire" covers many different types of emotions, craving is a particular form of desire, which Buddha identified as the cause of suffering. Not all forms of desire should lead to suffering but there are certain kinds of desire that we harbor or encourage in ourselves which then lead to the experience of suffering, to disappointment, and frustration. This happens precisely because our very act of craving does not correspond to how events are actually evolving. That for which we develop a craving, we crave for in such a manner that it goes against how things actually exist. Therefore, we get disappointed. We do not think, "This is reality." Rather, we think, "It didn't work out, but things are actually the way I think they are. It's just that this time I did not succeed. But if I try again, next time I will succeed." Buddha said it is like a moth leaping into a flame. It will continue to do so until it kills itself. We are on a similar kind of path.

So the cause of suffering is craving and because of craving, our ability to deal with the suffering of change and the suffering of suffering deteriorates. Our ability becomes more and more reduced. This does not mean that we suffer because things change. This is not the reason. Rather, we suffer because we think things ought to be different from how they are. The Buddha said that by understanding this, we learn how to moderate and manage our desires. We have to learn to see that certain desires are appropriate and necessary, even for survival, and also that other forms of desire are not necessary and are actually bad for our well-being.

Desire, Freedom, and Renunciation

In the previous chapter, I was not implying that renunciates do not renounce anything. I am not underplaying the sacrifices made by people who adopt the path of the ordained monk or nun. My point is that they are also exercising their own free will, their own choices. They are making decisions in such a manner that they think, "This particular lifestyle is more favorable for me, and if I adopt this lifestyle, I will grow more. I will flourish. But if I get married, settle down and have a family, the associated responsibilities, such as a mortgage, and so on, would mean that I wouldn't be able to focus attention on my interests and passions." I am not saying it has to be like this, but that people are different and have to make different choices and decisions. A person who has adopted a renunciate lifestyle still exercises choices, and making choices means that you have desires. You desire one option, and you do not desire the other option. It is very difficult to eradicate all forms of desire. This is not just a practical measure but, as the Buddha mentioned, it is necessary for us to curb our excessive desires, the craving that manifests in the form of greed or excessive attachment.

If we think like this, Buddha's notion of detachment makes sense. "Detachment" does not mean you are without interests, that you lead a disinterested life and so, therefore, your life is uninteresting, or that you lead a very uneventful and boring life because you do not have any preferences. This is not the Buddhist way. The Buddha said we should choose to have certain kinds of thoughts, emotions, and feelings, and learn to reduce certain other forms of thoughts and emotions. According to the Buddha, we do this by learning not to get too caught up in what we experience. The Buddha said that if we contemplate on this, we will get more understanding of what we can do and what we cannot do, especially in terms of our immediate future. When we follow the Buddhist path, we should think in terms of what we are capable of doing and then have an ideal notion of the person that we aim to become.

This then corresponds to what Buddhism says about ultimate happiness and temporal happiness. The teachings say that we should have a distant goal of attaining ultimate happiness (Tib. *thartuk gi dewa*) but in the immediate future, on a daily basis, we should learn to have experience of immediate or temporary happiness (Tib. *tral gyi dewa*). These two kinds of happiness are not pitted against each other, as some may believe. People may think Buddhism is saying that we should not pursue temporary happiness but rather should aim for ultimate happiness. This is not true. We could say a false kind of temporary happiness exists, but there is also a *genuine* temporary happiness that one can attain. The false happiness comes from, for example, getting pleasure out of indulging in negative emotions or actions. It may make us feel good for a time. It gives us a buzz for a short period of time but, in the long run, it has a harmful effect and does not make us happy. In fact, it adds to our misery. But the happiness we gain from cultivating ourselves in terms of our thoughts, feelings, emotions, conduct, and behavior, that happiness is genuine happiness. For example, if we do something nice for someone, which makes them happy, and seeing their happiness makes us happy, this kind of happiness is a good thing. It is genuine happiness and we should be happy. We should not be thinking, "I am a Buddhist and I should not feel really happy that I've done something helpful for somebody because this might inflate my ego. It may smack of selfishness." This relates to the idea of one's sense of selfhood as well because when we indulge in negative mental states and processes, it leads to the experience of disappointment and frustration. Therefore, at the heart of suffering is always the sense of an "I."

When Buddhism teaches us to be self-reflective, the idea is to actually look at ourselves as if somebody else is looking at us. We often think, "It's me who is having this or that experience. I am going through this. I am going through that." Instead of reviewing one's life or observing what is happening, we are always thinking, "I am having this experience. I am having that experience." Buddhism says because of that, the more negative thoughts and emotions begin to proliferate. This then accentuates one's egoism. The explanation given for this is that there is an unwillingness to accept what is really going on; one is thinking about how things ought to be. Due to things not working out the way we expect, we get frustrated and disappointed. This subsequently cements one's egoism because negative emotions are founded on unsatisfied desires and expectations. It is very unsettling, and one's sense of self becomes more and more threatened. The more threats that are perceived, the more one begins to react in a more desperate way, which then inflames the emotions and feelings even more. One gets caught up in a vicious circle. This, as I mentioned earlier, is called samsara or cyclic existence: repeating or reliving the same kinds of samsaric experiences over and over.

We do this all the time due to lack of wisdom or ignorance. Craving, according to Buddhism, is a way of trying to secure oneself, finding some kind of mooring or stable place, but it does not do that. It actually rebounds and is destabilizing and, because of this, samsara is described in many of the Buddhist texts as a fearful place. Everything we experience feels like some kind of threat, and a lot of these are perceived threats, not even real threats, according to the teachings. In our delusory mental state, we see all kinds of things as potential threats, and we react either with aggression, or with excessive craving and attachment. Either response is unhelpful. It only causes more paranoia and fear within us. This is how avoidable suffering is created. Therefore, we use the Dharma as the antidote to curb our excessive craving, and replace it with forms of desire that are helpful to our growth and in establishing our sense of identity.

Self-Identity

It may be surprising to hear that as Buddhists, we have to think about building our self-identity. Buddhism does not say we shouldn't establish a proper, stable sense of self-identity. Rather, Buddhism is against the idea that we already have a ready-made self, as though we just have to rediscover or recover it, that it is just there, waiting to be revealed. What Buddhism says is that we reconstruct our self all the time. Buddhist practice in itself is a form of refurbishing the different structural parts of the self we are building. Buddhism also says that we have to do this piecemeal, that to effect change in ourselves, we cannot overhaul ourselves in one stroke. We have to do it in stages, looking at what our weak points are, where our strengths are, and then using both. By using both our weak points and our strong points, we can actually reinvent ourselves.

This is why in Buddhist literature, three different kinds of individuals are spoken about: inferior, middling, and superior. Alternatively, we could speak about ordinary beings, extraordinary beings, and noble beings. Some may think these are elitist concepts, but they are not. Buddhism does not say only some people can attain these levels. Rather, it says that everybody should try to transform themselves, better themselves. If we do this, then we will become a different kind of person, but to achieve it we do not try to gradually peel away the outer layers to get to the kernel or core. According to Buddhism, this is not the way to look at it. Even the Tibetan word for "buddha" describes it. Buddha is translated as *sangyé*. Sangyé does not actually mean "buddha." Buddha means "awakened one." Sangyé is made up of two words: *sang* means "abandonment" and *gyé* means "expand." We attain sang when we abandon all the inhibiting factors that stop us reaching our full potential. Gyé means: "the complete, full expression of one's positive qualities or innate wholesome qualities." To reach this state, Buddhism speaks of abandoning all kinds of negative thoughts, feelings, and emotions, and refraining or disengaging from particular behaviors. We try to cultivate certain kinds of thoughts, emotions, and feelings, which are called "accumulations": the accumulation of merit and the accumulation of wisdom.

Merit and Wisdom

"Accumulation of merit" and "accumulation of wisdom" are generic terms that cover the different activities of body, speech, and mind that build merit and wisdom. Merit comes from performing generous acts that are conducive to our betterment. The idea is that if our actions of body, speech, and mind are conducted in a way that is genuinely conducive to our growth, it will naturally be beneficial for others. Whatever is good for us will also have a positive impact on others. Whatever is bad for us will impact negatively on others. Therefore, when we build merit with our body, speech, and mind, these are known as "accumulations." The accumulation of merit results from dealing with our affective aspect—emotions and feelings. Accumulation of wisdom comes through trying to organize our thoughts and to think clearly. This is dealing with one's cognitive aspect. We need to develop both.

We need to learn to free our mind from the emotions and feelings that drag us down or poison us. The negative emotions are toxic. They are not healthy and may even impact on our physical health. But just working on our negative emotions, in itself, is not sufficient. We also have to start to think in a different way. Even though we are trying our best to deal with our emotional side, if we have not really changed our mind, and still believe in all kinds of nonsense, our suffering will persist. We will not be free of suffering because it is not just the emotions that bring about suffering. Thinking improperly is the real culprit. This is the Buddhist view.

Craving is not even the true source of suffering. It is the symptom, which comes from mistaken beliefs or thinking incorrectly. The improper way of thinking leads to excessive craving but the accumulation of wisdom corrects this malady. It is an antidote to the improper way of thinking. As the Buddha has said, improper thinking is like getting caught up in a maze. It is hard to get ourselves out of the maze because the disorganized thoughts are jumbled together and lead us in different directions. We do not know where we are going or what we are doing. Sorting these out is important. We have to jettison, drop, or relieve ourselves of certain burdens we are carrying: the unresolved emotions, feelings, and distorted ways of thinking. At the same time as we lighten our load, we try to pick up more provisions, the things that we need on our path to enlightenment or nirvana.

Ego and Personality

By doing this, we develop a new identity, a new personality. Buddhism does not say we should not have an identity, a personality. The idea of egolessness or selflessness can be misinterpreted in that way. Contrary to reality, we think there is something inside called the "self" or "ego" remaining hidden or aloof, like a pilot in the cockpit or a driver behind the vehicle. However, Buddhism does not believe in this. Buddhism believes that we are made up of different elements. In weaning ourselves off certain aspects of that which is contrary to reality, they will dry up or perish. Then we should nurture those qualities that we need on the path to enlightenment. As it is said in Buddhist teachings, if we put manure and water in the areas that we need to develop, in due course we will become a different kind of person. We will be transformed. Self-transformation occurs in that way.

If we look at Buddhist teachings on the paths and stages, we will see that it is sometimes described in a very precise manner. But whether it actually happens like that or not, we do not have to be bothered too much. What is important is that if we get to a particular level, then we will have dropped off many kinds of inhibiting mental restrictions and constraints. We will have opened up more abilities, capacities, things that we did not have before. The paths and stages are described like that.

Again, this means that self-transformation happens in a piecemeal fashion. If we work with the negative aspects, it does not mean that they will all disappear simultaneously. Some negative aspects will be more virulent or more persistent; others will be easier to manage and overcome. Similarly, on the other side, certain qualities might be more challenging to develop for the individual concerned, and other qualities may be less so. For example, people may have certain issues with anger, but not have many problems with miserliness. Somebody may have a quick or volatile temper, but a generous nature. On one level, we have aspects that we need to work more with, and other aspects, less so.

This is important because somebody may have been doing meditation for some time and think, "Well, I've been doing meditation for five years and I don't see much change." However, this is the incorrect way to think. Just because we do Buddhist meditation practice does not mean all the unpleasantness of life will just disappear. The point is that until we attain full enlightenment, until we become a buddha, there will always be something that we have to work on.

Transformation

This is the view in Mahayana Buddhism. Until they reach enlightenment, even the most advanced *bodhisattvas*[24] have something to renounce, jettison, or get rid of since they do not possess the positive qualities equal to those of a fully enlightened buddha. This is a very encouraging model for the spiritual seeker. It says that a quite spiritually advanced individual may still have features that are not completely edifying. They may still have issues to work with. This is important since we may often think that doing meditation is about attaining perfection, that we become completely flawless. It is not that we become flawless immediately, but we become more adept at dealing with our circumstances, situations, and our mental states and processes.

Therefore, because our mind is in a less tormented state, to put it in Buddhist terms, we are transforming as a person. This is the main goal. The main goal in the immediate future is not to become perfect. Perfection is an ideal that we aim towards but, like the goal of happiness in the near future, it is not about perfection; it is about becoming more adept. One becomes more accomplished in dealing with one's unpleasant experiences in life. When we go through ups and downs we should not give in to samsaric experiences in a very unreflective fashion. If we do not submit to these experiences but can deal with them in the proper way, we are becoming transformed. This is the yardstick or measuring instrument. The gauge is not about whether "I still feel angry," "I still feel disappointed," or "I still feel depressed," but it is about the extent to which these impact on our life. In other words, it is not black and white.

With regard to so-called positive emotions and feelings, and negative emotions and feelings, we do not see them as separate entities in two different baskets. They should be seen as the two ends of one continuum. At the extreme end, we have purely positive thoughts, and, at the other end, purely negative thoughts. Gradually, as we move to the middle, it becomes more grey or mixed. As we go further away from the middle, it becomes either more positive or more negative.

When we transform ourselves, the transformation occurs in a similar way. This relates to what was said earlier about these things happening in a piecemeal way and not in stages. When we speak of "stages," it means that everything happens at the same level at each stage, rather than everything happening at different levels at the same stage. It is like this even in relation to our meditation practices, our practice of meditative concentration. Whatever level of meditative concentration one attains, it happens in a similar way. So simply because one has thoughts and emotions, it does not mean one is not in a meditative state of concentration, as we may sometimes think. Self-transformation occurs in that way because we are getting better at managing our desires and we are learning to curb our craving. Because of this, we can enjoy our lives more and have more experiences of happiness.

Courage, Strength, Fortitude, Resilience

In Buddhism, happiness does not mean we do not have pain or do not have unhappiness. "Happiness" understood in this way means that even when we are unhappy, the intensity of that unhappiness does not become overwhelming. In that sense, we are still happy. "Happiness," from the Buddhist point of view, does not mean that all pain will disappear, but that we have a cheerful or positive outlook and do not plunge into a defeatist attitude, thinking that things are too difficult or overwhelming. Rather, our attitude is always to think that things can be done, things can be achieved. In Mahayana, there are many stories of bodhisattvas, like Chenrezig,[25] for example, not giving up, always trying, and thinking that things can be achieved. By having such an attitude, one becomes a stronger person. Even though Buddhism talks about "selflessness" or "egolessness," it also talks about the strength of the self, the individual, and this is seen as very important. Notions of courage, strength, fortitude, resilience—we are instructed to develop these qualities because if we suffer a setback, but have resilience, we do not give up. We bounce back. If we have fortitude when things get rough, we do not throw our arms in the air, or start breaking down, having a meltdown. If we have courage, even if we think there is a difficult and challenging task, we do not shy away from it or cringe. We do our best. We give it a shot. By doing this, we become stronger as individuals. We can advance more this way than by following our normal egoistic tendencies by asserting a sense of dominance. Such an approach does not work. As Buddhism says, when we try to dominate, we become weaker, more paranoid, more fearful, less courageous, and less resilient. In some ways, we become sicker. This is why Dharma is seen as the medicine, Buddha as the doctor, and we as the patients. We are made sicker by our afflictions.

I want to emphasize in this chapter the idea of dealing with suffering in such a manner that we become stronger as individuals. Thinking along these lines is helpful in terms of transforming ourselves. Rather than thinking that there is already a self to be discovered, what we are is a work in progress. Buddhism says this, and this is how we should see ourselves, because then we can think about how to become the person we want to become. This is a very practical approach. We can literally see it. We can see certain aspects of ourselves that we need to work on, in terms of our weaknesses and strengths. If we look at it like this, everything becomes doable; otherwise it remains undoable, overwhelming. If we look at it in terms of doing this in piecemeal fashion, then everything becomes manageable, practical, attainable, within reach, and not at all abstract.

6
Noble Eightfold Path

The eightfold path is as follows:
1. Right view
2. Right intention or contemplation
3. Right speech
4. Right action
5. Right livelihood
6. Right effort
7. Right mindfulness
8. Right concentration

Understanding why we should follow the Dharma or practice Buddhism is obviously very important, irrespective of which practices may be involved. Unless we are interested only in creating positive karma in order to have more immediate comfort in life, in Buddhism, if we want to have genuine relief from suffering, the practices we do and the way we practice them, must be orientated towards liberation. In Buddhism, we make a distinction between liberation and full enlightenment, which means that even if we do not attain full enlightenment, we can still find liberation from the cycle of samsaric pain and suffering.

This is why, if we are really practicing, we cannot separate Buddhist philosophy from Buddhist practice. The subject matter we have covered so far, lays the foundation for the Buddhist philosophy of life, both in terms of theory and of practice because theory and practice cannot be separated. This is made very clear in the way that the noble eightfold path is presented. The way out of suffering, according to the Buddha, is to follow the noble eightfold path, which is the fourth noble truth. At the very beginning, Buddha establishes right view as the first part of the noble eightfold path.

It is necessary to have the right view because not understanding how things actually are and how they work, produces craving and, because of craving, we experience suffering. But craving exists in the first place because we do not have the correct understanding of how things work. Trying to understand how they work is extremely important. Therefore, to think in that way is not just a theoretical or intellectual exercise, but also an essential philosophical reflection, in order to produce wisdom.

The second part of the noble eightfold path is right intention or right contemplation. This means that one actually has to think about or reflect on things in the proper manner. So right view has to be supported by right intention. In other words, one engages in these reflections in the proper fashion.

"Right speech" basically means we do not spend time gossiping, engaging in idle chatter, or pitting friends against each other by saying one thing to one of them and something different to the other to cause friction. Misleading people by being untruthful is also mentioned. These examples are all called "wrong speech." To use right speech is to try to mend the friction between two people in conflict and to try to speak truthfully in a skillful fashion.

"Right action" means not performing harmful actions or using one's body in an inappropriate fashion, for example, striking somebody.

According to Buddhism, "right livelihood" means we do not make a living from something that would cause direct harm to other beings—for example, working in a butcher's shop or in an ammunition factory. Dealing in poisons and other harmful substances is also said to be wrong livelihood. Barring these kinds of occupations, one is free to make one's own living, according to Buddhism. For example, running a business is not seen in a negative way, although, of course, as a businessperson, one must be honest in one's business dealings. In Buddhism, there is not the idea that just by being in business you cannot be an honest person; that it is a wrong livelihood, as some people may believe. Obviously, Buddha was not of that opinion because he had many merchants and businesspeople among his followers. This is also in the sutras. Therefore, right livelihood has to do with making a living that does not bring harm to others, and this is important.

After that, is right effort. According to Buddhism, laziness is seen in a negative light. Basically, it is said that if we do not use our time in a productive way, we are wasting our life. We have a very short life and, before we know it, we have squandered our life away. It is very important to make the most of our time and not be complacent.

"Right mindfulness" means training our mind in such a way that we pay attention to what is going on in our life and, as a result, we learn what to forget and what to remember. It is not often explained this way but, in Buddhism, this is the meaning of "mindfulness" (Skt. *smriti*; Tib. *drenpa*). The word, "mindfulness" literally means "remembrance." "Remembering to forget" is also mentioned, as is "remembering not to forget," "to retain." Both are accomplished through the practice of mindfulness. Earlier, we discussed how to renounce certain aspects of ourselves, to free ourselves from them. This is a way of learning to forget and let go of certain things. We also covered accumulation of merit, which is an exercise in remembrance. Nurturing that which actually supports and is helpful to us is an exercise in remembrance. It is through remembrance that we learn to make these practices more a part of ourselves.

Right concentration comes from the practice of mindfulness. This obviously means we learn to deal with our distractions when they arise so that we become more skillful in being able to concentrate and just focus on what we need to focus on. Concentration is a practice. As we become better at it, we are able to better maintain concentration in a variety of situations. In the beginning, we may be able to practice concentration only in a certain environment or in certain situations, such as sitting on the cushion during meditation. Then, gradually, we might be able to concentrate in other situations, such as reading, driving, and talking to people. Often we find this very difficult but we learn to focus; we are right there. When we are at work or even when we are speaking to somebody, we find it difficult to concentrate fully on our task or on what the person is saying. Basically, we learn to concentrate in a variety of situations, and although we start from a very feeble beginning, we then reach a more established level of concentration. In other words, it is a form of mind-training. When the mind becomes habituated to operate in a certain way, it automatically functions in that manner. If concentration becomes a mental habit, then it becomes easy. As it is said in the Mahayana teachings, "There is nothing that does not become easier through practice."

This is what Buddha said we should do, in terms of dealing with our current situation and our suffering, and learning what the antidotes are. As we can see, Buddha says that we actually need to deal with the body, speech, and mind—all three. We need to bring about change on all three levels. Even though Buddhism emphasizes the mind, simply working on the mind itself is not sufficient. We have to work on our speech and on our body. All three aspects have to be worked on.

In light of that, we can see with the development of Buddhism, how Buddhist yoga and medicine would have been an extension of practices associated with working with body, speech, and mind. In other words, Buddha may not have spoken explicitly about these practices but, nevertheless, he spoke of the need to work on body, speech, and mind. Since, later on, Mahayana Buddhism started to incorporate different vocal and physical exercises, and developed elaborate meditational practices involving extensive visualization, we can see how this may then relate to working with body, speech, and mind.

7
Foundations of Wisdom

The Buddha said that we suffer because of craving, which arises due to ignorance. Ignorance occurs because we do not have proper understanding and it is because of this that craving is there. But what did Buddha mean by, "We do not understand things as they are?" He said that nothing has real enduring substance. Everything is subject to change. This was one of his main messages: nothing lasts, everything is subject to change so, therefore, craving is harmful. Because everything changes and nothing lasts, therefore, to have strong craving leads to the experience of suffering. Due to craving—clinging, grasping, and excessive attachment then follow. Because of this, our mind becomes disturbed. The Buddha spoke about this and it was later elaborated upon. The Buddha said that we do not understand how things work or, indeed, how we work and we get confused because of that.

How is it that we do not understand ourselves? Buddha did not think that this lack of self-understanding was anything to do with not understanding our true self. He thought that it was to do with our not knowing how the different parts of us are interconnected, how they function in relationship to each other. Not understanding how our thoughts, emotions, feelings, and our physicality are interconnected gives us the wrong picture of what we are, what we are like. Our lack of understanding then, has to do with our failure to understand these relationships, rather than our inability to understand our self, in the sense of some kind of hidden self. It is not that we are fixated on a false empirical or conventional notion of the self, that we have lost sight of the true self, and that our job is to retrieve it and try to move away or detach ourselves from the false self. Buddha did not think in those terms. He thought that what was not understood was what we already experience, in relation to ourselves.

By understanding more about what we already experience, we gain self-knowledge—for example, how our thoughts impact on our emotions, how our emotions and feelings are tied up together, and how our physical states relate to our mental states. This is why, in meditation, we focus our mind on our breathing. According to the Buddha, whatever our mental state is, our physical response is also there. Our posture, whether the body is relaxed or rigid, and our level of physical health—these are interrelated. Through understanding ourselves in relation to these, we will understand ourselves better.

Craving, Beauty, and Dharmas

The same applies to what we experience in terms of the world. We think there are objects called tables, chairs, mountains, and so on. The Buddha said, "To develop wisdom, we need to analyze." We may wish to understand an object or how certain things work. To use a modern example, if we want to see how a watch works then we open it up, take out the parts, and see how they all work together. Then we will be able to see how the watch works. The Buddha called everything we perceive *dharmas*. Even the teachings are called "Dharma" because through understanding the dharmas, we understand Buddha's teachings. This is because Buddha's teachings described the dharmas. So the different mental and physical elements are called "dharmas." To gain insight into how things work, we have to understand the interconnected nature of dharmas, how the various mental and physical entities work together. I will discuss dharmas in further detail in the section on

Buddhist philosophy.

Therefore, craving arises from looking at phenomena as unified entities—"a person," "a table," or "a chair." For example, by seeing the form of a beautiful object, extreme craving or desire arises because what we see is a single entity. However, by breaking it into elements, we get a better picture of the whole and this helps us reduce our craving. The first impression sucks us in but if we take a moment and try, mentally or physically, to break things down, then we will have a better picture of how they work. By doing so, our craving will be reduced.

Buddha was not saying we should not be attracted to beautiful objects. Buddha was not against our finding certain phenomena beautiful or attractive. What the Buddha saw as the problem was when the reaction to certain objects is disproportionate to the object itself, whether it is attraction or aversion. This is what Buddha meant when he spoke about strong attachment, grasping, or clinging; it is not about the fact that we find certain things attractive. For this reason, Buddha devised many different kinds of meditation practices, depending on what people needed to work with. For somebody with extreme lust, he told them to meditate on skeletons and to regard bodies as foul. For somebody who had problems with anger, he told them to meditate on colored objects, such as blue circles. For people who were suffering from ignorance, he spoke about dependent origination.

In any case, the meditation on the foulness of the body which I referred to is often misinterpreted and so people say that Buddha was very much against things being regarded as attractive or desirable. Buddha was not against something being seen as attractive as long as one realizes that what one is seeing is the product of causes and conditions. Since it is the product of causes and conditions, decay is built into whatever we come across. Seeing this is all that is necessary. Seeing something as beautiful is not the problem. If one sees something as being beautiful, while knowing it to be transient and the product of causes and conditions then, according to the Buddha, one has a better perspective. Therefore, the craving will be lessened.

In Japan, for example, this idea is incorporated into the Japanese psyche. The chrysanthemum became a symbol of the beauty that lasts for only a short time. Because of its transiency, its beauty is accentuated. Something attractive that goes on and on and on may not be considered as beautiful as something like a chrysanthemum, which is so delicate, so ephemeral. The Buddha is giving us a perspective on how things are and how they operate. Buddha's prescription for how we should conduct ourselves is based on this understanding. Buddhist ethics, too, are based on the understanding that all things are interconnected. How we see ourselves, the agent, being in the world, and the world that surrounds us, all depend on understanding this one concept: that everything is composed of elements.

With regard to the mind or to consciousness, instead of thinking, "I have a mind," in Buddhism we ponder: "What does this mean? What is this consciousness?" This is based on introspection. Buddha asked, "What do we see when we engage in introspection?" Obviously, we have a lot of information coming through our senses: our visual sense, our audial sense, our nasal sense, our tactile sense, and so on, and we have the sense organs. According to the Buddha, there is not just a sense organ that registers what one perceives but there is a consciousness that is allied with each respective sense. When we see something, the visual consciousness recognizes what one perceives, and it is the same with the rest of the senses. The sixth consciousness, the thinking mind, subsequently organizes all of this into coherent form. This is called "primary mind," in Buddhism. Primary mind, in turn, is supported by what we call "secondary mind," sometimes translated, perhaps inaccurately, as "mental events." Secondary mind involves various mental states and processes that we are all familiar with. Some are operating and more manifest and some are dormant. These supporting mental mechanisms are responsible for producing either pleasant or unpleasant experiences and for producing the kind of character we have, the kind of person we become. It is also tied up with our personalities, dispositions, and our psychic tendencies.

Interrelationship and Is-ness

When we do meditation, we are sometimes instructed to notice how the elements work together. At other times we are instructed to cultivate some aspects and discourage others. I will talk about this in a later chapter but, at this point, I would like to emphasize how important it is in Buddhism to understand things in terms of relationships and not entities. Instead of trying to see the *is-ness* of something, we try to understand it in terms of what it is related to or dependent on. In other words, even though we analyze and think in terms of different elements, we do not think of them in isolation, but look at them in terms of their relationship to other elements.

When you examine a clock, you do not look at the particular part in terms of its is-ness. What it is, is less important than what it does, in relation to the other parts. If we understand what its job is, relative to what the other parts are doing, then we understand it better. Similarly, with our mind, if we understand our thoughts, emotions, and feelings when they occur, and can see their individual connections with the others, we gain a better understanding of a particular thought, emotion, or feeling because we can see how it operates. In other words, the cultivation of wisdom does not come from trying to see the is-ness of things and Buddhism is not about that. Often, when we talk about gaining insight or knowledge, we think in terms of is-ness, what its substance is, what it *really* is. However, according to Buddhism, nothing is like that. For example, even with language, we try to understand a word in terms of a definition. We try to define a word, we try to understand what that word means through definition. According to Buddhism, unlike the words in the dictionary, which are static, already written, and finished, if we look at the objects the words refer to, then we can see that the process is not as clear-cut as we think. We try to make it clear-cut because it is neat and it helps us to pigeonhole and classify. In reality it is actually to do with something being more like, or less like, something else. According to Buddhism, this is an enormous insight because it means that nothing is what it is, in itself. It is what it is because of something else; because other things are similar or dissimilar or even very different from it.

Fixation and Misunderstanding

This is not simply some idle philosophy. It is a very practical philosophy that will help us understand how things work, how things are, and, because of this, we will not be so fixated on things. In Tibetan Buddhism and in Buddhism generally, the word "fixation" is frequently used. "Fixation" in Buddhism, unlike in psychoanalysis, means latching on to whatever we experience; but what we latch on to is the idea of an object or experience, not the object itself. It is just an idea. In Buddhism, then, it is said that when we become fixated on something, we are, in fact, fixating on an idea.

For example, we may have an idea of "humanity" or "justice" but, in reality, there are only individual human beings. Buddhism makes a distinction between our individual experience of things and our conceptual understanding of things. In our unreflective mode, we get these two mixed up. Due to this, we become fixated on certain ideas. We seize upon these ideas and we cannot let go of them. This is a clear example of how craving manifests itself. We fix on to an idea, but whatever the idea is, it always changes. It has moved on but we have not and this is the problem. There is discrepancy or incongruity between our own individual experiences and *that which we have experience of*. The result is suffering because there is no match. What is actually happening is totally different from what we think is happening.

That is why we are taught in Buddhism not to conceptualize too much. This does not mean that we should not be thinking, as some people interpret it to mean. It means we should try to pay more attention, on a continuous basis, to our experience, rather than trying to fit our experiences into pre-established categories of thought. In other words, it is said that we already have a filing cabinet and, as we get older, the filing cabinet gets larger and larger and has more and more drawers with different labels. Buddhist teachers say that, of course, this is useful, but we should think of using our concepts and ideas more pragmatically. It may be a useful tool, but it is only a tool and that, according to Buddhism, is our mistake. We think it is actually a mirror and that whatever we are thinking is a true reflection of how things are.

There are degrees of reality. In Buddhism, the concept, "humanity" is the least real. It does not correspond to anything real in the outside world. The concept "human beings" has more reality, but even that is not so very real. Individuals' thoughts, emotions, feelings, physical states, and processes do have more reality than the idea of human beings but the thoughts and emotions and so on, of course, are not ultimately real. In other words, the more abstract a concept, the less reality it has, and the more concrete the concept, the more reality. This is the Buddhist view.

Mindfulness and Interdependent Origination

The practice of mindfulness has importance because, through practicing mindfulness, we are able to detect the various elements and how they interact so that we become aware of each thought that arises, each emotion that arises, and each mood that arises in us. Through this, we may realize that we need to work more on a particular aspect or difficulty, for example, and we remember to do that. We may then detect other issues that we need to work on, in terms of letting go or overcoming them. Subsequently, we remember to do these things as well. This is how we practice mindfulness and cultivate wisdom.

According to the Buddha, this is how we come to understand interdependent origination. He said that the thinking of most people falls into one of two extremes. One extreme is to think, "This world is illusory. The self that I experience now is illusory, but there is a divine reality beneath the changing face of the world that I perceive, and that reality is eternal." Similarly, "What I experience on a daily basis is my false self, but I have another self, which is unchanging, atman,[26] and that is real." Buddha said that this is one extreme and he referred to the group who hold this view as the "eternalists." He spoke also of others who reflect on such matters, whose belief is, "Nothing is actually real. Nothing exists." This group falls into the nihilistic extreme.

By understanding things in the way we have been discussing, we arrive at the middle way. The middle way, as taught by the Buddha, is what interdependent origination represents. With this approach, we do not fall into the extremes of nihilism or eternalism. We do not assert there is a self, so we do not fall into the extreme of believing in self or soul as some kind of psychic substance that is immutable, unchanging, and permanent. On the other hand, we do not say that there is no self, that there is nothing, no agent, no karma, no ethics, or no morality—that anything goes. The Buddha identified this as the nihilistic extreme, so we do not go there either.

So to understand interdependent origination, which represents the middle view, we think about it in those terms. Everything that we experience comes about due to causes and conditions. The thoughts that we have, the emotions that we have, do not happen in a vacuum. When we recognize this we can see how to free ourselves from what binds us; we also realize that we have the capacity to develop what is needed. Buddha thought that in seeing things this way he had gained a great insight. He felt that with this understanding, we could bring about the experiences we wish to have but have not yet gained. How? Since everything is dependent on causes and conditions then, through our own willpower, we can create the appropriate causes and conditions, which, once present, will deliver the desired experiences. If not for interdependent origination, it would be out of our hands.

Since everything is dependent on causes and conditions, conversely, we can learn to free ourselves from the things we do not desire and want to be free of. How? We can achieve this by trying not to contribute to the persistence of causes and conditions that promote them, and trying one's best not to encourage them. This was Buddha's view. He thought this really gives one a sense of agency and willpower, to take charge of one's life. Some people believe that subscribing to the idea that everything comes about through causes and conditions would compromise our sense of free will. They say that if everything is the product of causes and conditions, then these causes and conditions would have supervenience[27] over one's sense of agency. This is not how Buddha felt. He thought it was completely the opposite insofar as, since things are the product of causes and conditions, we have the chance to assert our own free will, the chance to make things happen. So we create the causes and conditions, just as in life generally: if we want something, we try to create those causes and conditions.

This is how Buddha felt about karma as well. Karma is a product of causes and conditions so we have inherited our karma from the past. It is inherited from the past, but the future of one's karma is not predetermined; we can change our course. The past does not determine our future. It has an impact on our present but, in the present, we have the chance of changing our course. There is no reason why we should continue what we have been doing in the past. So, as far as Buddha was concerned, causality is not an impediment since we have free will and can change or transform ourselves. We can do things differently and live differently, have a different life. Buddha did not see any incompatibility, probably because he did not speak only about cause and effect but always included the idea of conditions. The cause and effect relationship is not so tight that, even if there are certain causes, a particular effect will invariably arise. There are extraneous or mitigating circumstances and situations present in any given context. Therefore, the Buddha thought that when it comes to creating favorable situations, if past negative experiences threaten the possibility of our having the positive experiences we expect, then we can undertake preemptive measures to de-potentiate the effects of negative experiences. Those negative experiences will not then have an adverse effect and prevent us having the positive experiences we want. This is how we can nullify the karmic effects of past experiences.

In speaking about the interrelationships of dharmas, including the concept of karma, we can see that this relationship is real and that it works that way. How the elements interact and mutually influence each other, however, is not pre-established. There is fluidity and elasticity and we can see the patterns forming, but how they operate is not pre-established. With regard to the parts they play and how they operate, there is always variance or difference and, because of that, it is possible to make our life better and reduce our suffering. This is the Buddhist view. So because things come about through causes and conditions, by understanding these causes and conditions, we can learn how to make things happen— or not happen— as the case may be.

Secondly, even though networks of causal relationships occur on many different levels—on the physical and mental levels—there is still much room for movement. Because things are not pre-established, preordained, or predetermined, there is great flexibility and, as a result, we can make things happen. We can change things; we are not tied to our past. In fact, according to the Buddha, we can even change our past from the standpoint of the present. We can change our past and our future course. According to the Buddha, the present is not a slice of time that stands by itself. The present carries the past with it and it is also oriented towards the future. If it were not like this, then we could not explain karma; we would be at a loss to explain karma. Because the present carries the past, karma is there. Since the past is there as part of the present, one can also change the past, in terms of past influences. Simply because one had certain experiences in the past, does not mean that it is a case of: "Now it has happened and nothing can be done about it." The past can be remedied in some ways.

Wisdom

What is wisdom and what do Buddhists mean by "wisdom?" The wisdom comes from seeing the relationships: not perceiving everything in terms of separate entities in isolation, but trying to view a given element in relation to other components. This gives us a better understanding. It is like trying to understand a concept or idea or even a word in a book, in relation to its context. If we put the word in context, we see so much more than when we look at the word itself in isolation. Similarly, when we try to grasp an idea in isolation, we will learn less than if we put that idea in context. It is the same with a statement someone has made. In isolation, we may interpret the statement in a particular way but, if we put it in context, we may even see that the meaning of the statement changes. Seeing it in that way is called "wisdom," according to Buddhism. This way of looking at it is very important, and it permeates all aspects of Buddhism, including ethics, morality, yoga, and Tibetan medicine, which we will discuss in subsequent chapters.

Section Two
Philosophy

8
Why Integrate Philosophy?

We may not think of Buddhism as having much to offer in relation to the variety of aspects that comprise our life generally, but it allows us to pick and choose. If, for example, somebody were intellectually inclined, they may choose to study Buddhist philosophy but meditation may not hold any appeal. Somebody who is attracted to Buddhist meditation may have zero interest in Buddhist philosophy and Buddhist psychology. There are people who have university degrees in Buddhist philosophy, but they may never have meditated, even for ten minutes, in their entire life. It happens like that.

If we read Buddhist literature, we may think that some meditators hated philosophy and intellectuals. Of course, for some meditators, philosophy was not the most important aspect. There is much criticism leveled at Buddhist philosophers and intellectuals, but we need to put this in context. Many traditional Buddhist masters and meditators were also quite well-versed in philosophy. Within Zen Buddhism, for example, this was the case, yet, in the West, Zen Buddhism has often been seen as having the most anti-intellectual of Buddhist practices. Indeed, the Zen approach does focus on direct experience but the great Chan masters of China and the Zen masters of Japan were very well versed in Confucian philosophy and linguistics and could read the Chinese classics in ancient Chinese.

In Buddhism, education has always been valued. Through education we have knowledge, and knowledge equals power. It is a self-empowering experience. What we know, we know. If we know how to look after ourselves physically, we have the knowledge of what to eat and what not to eat, how to exercise—not exercising too much, nor exercising too little, and so on. In any case, if we are armed with the right kind of knowledge, we can avoid adverse and undesirable things in our lives.

Buddhist philosophy, in that respect, has a practical dimension. Buddhist philosophy does not involve just thinking about abstract things and indulging in idle speculation. Buddhist philosophy, if we think about it properly, is basically practical philosophy. Learning a little about Buddhist philosophy will then allow us to see the world in a different way.

For example, we may decide to try to change our life around through sheer willpower, to behave in a different way but, in the end, it is not going to work. Unless there has been a shift in our cognitive structure, in terms of our brain or mind, we will not see things in a different way. If we do not see things differently, then trying to do things differently, simply using willpower, will not work. Because we still see things in the same way as before, there will be no change, no freshness. There is nothing new going in. Even when we experience new things, we still process and filter the new experiences through the same processing mechanism. The same old machine is used to process the information. While this takes place, the new information is then transformed and adulterated and comes out the same as before, since there has been no change in the cognitive structure. We will discuss this in a later chapter, in more detail.

Buddhist philosophy then, teaches us to look at things in a different way. We should not think, "Buddhist philosophy does not really teach anything practical. It is too intellectual. What is emptiness? 'Empty, empty, everything is empty.' So what? Big deal. I still have to pay my mortgage and show up at work five days a week." We may think, "Emptiness doesn't help. It does no good." However, that is not how we should think about it, because Buddhist philosophy, like a therapy, tries to help us think in different ways so that our thinking habit becomes more fluid. How do we think normally? Normally, for us, there is thought and there is reality, and thought and reality are fixed. Whatever we believe is going on, as far as we are concerned, is going on. It does not matter whether what is taking place corresponds to our thought or not. The belief in our head is, "Something or other is going on," and we think it is really happening. For example, we may get the idea, "My spouse is cheating on me" and that becomes reality—that is the reality. Alternatively, somebody cuts us off on the road when we are driving and we think this person wants to do harm to us. These are the kinds of things that we experience. We do not realize.

Values

Normally we make a distinction between fact and value, "fact," meaning *what is actually the case* and "value," meaning *what ought to be* or *should be the case*. When we think of something as factual but it is not factual, it is the result of a process imbued with values. In terms of the use of language, for what we see as actually being the case, we may use descriptive language, and for what we think ought to be, or should be the case, we may use prescriptive language. Prescriptive language would include examples such as: "I should do this" "I should do that," or "You ought to do this" "You ought to do that," etcetera. But when we encounter "factual" situations, we think, "Oh, I am just describing what is occurring." We are unaware of the evaluative judgments that we attribute to "factual" situations. We think that something is good, something is bad, that so and so is doing this, and so and so is doing that. We jump to conclusions. We generalize. We exaggerate. We do these kinds of things all the time.

We are not seeing reality and, due to our habits, as Buddhists would say, even when things are not the same as before, we think that the same thing is happening again. We end up having déjà vu experiences all the time, but we may not be revisiting the same old thing. If we could get a little more distant from what is happening, we might actually see it in a different light. It is not the same and we will see that and then be able to say, "It is not the same." It is because we are all riled up, and our mind or brain has become so wired to think in a particular way, that we see different or dissimilar things as being the same. Simply because certain situations or incidents in life resemble each other, does not mean they are the same because nothing is the same. They are not the same and not seeing them as being different limits us. Buddhist philosophy says that we limit ourselves when we do not pay attention to how we look at things, see things, and how we process the information that we receive from the external world, in relation to people, circumstances, situations, and the world generally.

We also need to pay attention to how we process the information we get through our senses and our intellectual and cognitive processes. In Buddhism, we emphasize the idea that much of the information we receive about the world is gathered through the senses, but not everything we think about is based on that. We also think about things that we have not seen, smelt, tasted, or touched, but which may still be true. For example, when we look at the idea, two and two equals four, we have not seen it, tasted it, smelt it, or touched it, but it has some kind of reality of its own. The main point I want to make is that what we think of as being real is contingent on our mind. Buddhism emphasizes that.

9
Abhidharma (Pali: Abhidhamma)

We will continue the discussion on the reasons the Buddha gave for following the Dharma. According to tradition, the Buddha said, "Whoever sees the Dharma, sees me." This is taken to mean that Buddha became a buddha because he realized the Dharma. In other words, it is not that Dharma is to be taken seriously because it was the Buddha who taught the Dharma. Buddha taught the Dharma because he realized the Dharma himself, and it was through realizing the Dharma that he became Shakyamuni Buddha.[28]

As it is said in early Buddhism, and especially in Mahayana Buddhism, there were buddhas before Shakyamuni Buddha, so Shakyamuni Buddha was not unique in that sense. In Mahayana Buddhism, we have the idea that there are many buddhas. There were many buddhas before Shakyamuni and there are many more to come. Each time a new buddha appears, the Dharma is being rediscovered. In other words, the truth of the Dharma is atemporal, and it is the same Dharma that each buddha realizes. Of course, how that Dharma is subsequently communicated and taught may vary for a number of reasons, one of which would be the buddha's own personality since each buddha would naturally have a unique way of communicating that body of truth known as "the Dharma."

It is in that way, in Buddhism, that we think of the Dharma as being even more important than the Buddha. For example, in Tibetan Buddhism, we are instructed not to put a statue of the

Buddha on top of a text. Although both texts and statues are merely representations of the Dharma and Buddha respectively, nevertheless, it is inappropriate and, to an extent, sacrilegious to place a statue on top of a text because of the sanctity of the Dharma. This Dharma is the antidote we need in order to work with our condition so that our suffering becomes more manageable and, in the long run, is overcome.

We have been speaking about this in relation to early Buddhism, and we have seen how the Buddhist philosophical contemplations aid us in reducing our clinging and craving. They also help us eliminate or clarify the confusion caused by ignorance (Skt. *avidya*). Avidya means "ignorance." *Vidya* is "insight" or "knowledge," and the "a" particle is negative, so avidya means "lack of knowledge" or "lack of insight" (Tib. *timuk*).

After Buddha passed away, Buddhist councils were convened in order to systematize Buddha's teachings. In time, the teachings were gathered together into three different categories, known as the Sutra, Vinaya, and Abhidharma (Pali: *Abhidhamma*) collections. The Sutra collection represents the original discourses of the Buddha and the Vinaya is the collection of texts setting out monastic rules for monks and nuns. These two collections are universally recognized as being the oldest of the Buddhist texts. The Abhidharma collection was then added to the other two. The Abhidharma comprises the commentaries on the essential content in the teachings contained in the Sutra collection, in particular, and to an extent in the Vinaya collection. These three are called *Tripitaka*, literally meaning "three baskets."

Mahayana Buddhism offers three different philosophical theories about reality. First, there is the early Buddhist theory of the Abhidharma where the idea of irreducible dharmas is spoken about. Dharmas mean "irreducible entities," and they are not just physical, but mental as well. On the physical level, atoms would be seen as dharmas and mentally, each thought we have is a dharma so, in the Abhidharma, the building block of reality is called "dharma." *Abhi* means "making obvious," so through the study of Abhidharma, we learn to make these dharmas obvious. We begin to understand how these dharmas work.

In Buddhism, we talk about two levels of truth. Therefore, from the Abhidharma point of view, when we see a table or a chair, they will have only relative reality because how the atoms are arranged, the configuration of the atoms, will be in the shape of a "table" or a "chair." It is relative so instead of being round, the table could have been square or it could have been shorter than it is. However, what the table is made of, the substance, does not change. It would be the same whether it was round, square, or had a different color. It would not make any difference. That is why they are called the "dharmas" and this is the absolute truth, according to Abhidharma. The absolute truth about the table is what it is made of, its essential substance (Skt. *dravya*; Tib. *dze*). The substance consists of the essential physical qualities of the object. It is the same with the mind. We have a mind, but the mind is made up of entities, according to Abhidharma, so that a thought, an emotion, or a feeling are also called "dharmas." Without them, there would be no mind. Therefore, mind has only relative reality, but the mental events or mental states have more reality than the mind taken as a whole. If you cannot think, imagine, remember, feel, anticipate or expect things to happen, or if you cannot dream, then you have no mind. You are gone. This is the kind of logic the Abhidharmists use.

According to Abhidharma teachings, we then have to realize that thoughts, emotions, feelings, and the dharmas—in a table, for instance—all these entities are not like monads,[29] closed unto themselves like billiard balls. Rather, the dharmas interact with each other so that they support the whole structure. It is the same in regard to the mind, where our thoughts, emotions, and feelings crisscross and interact with each other to create the mental life that we have. Similarly, the brain is not just a brain. There is the temporal lobe, frontal lobe, left hemisphere, right hemisphere, motor cortex, somatosensory cortex, parietal lobe, occipital lobe, cerebellum, the brain stem at the base, and the spinal cord. For the brain to function properly, we need all of these dharmas. We can refer to each one as a "dharma." With all these dharmas working together, we have a functioning brain. All the parts have to play their role. Impairment in a given part could, for example, affect our linguistic skills, learning capacity, or memory.

The idea of dharmas has to be understood as functioning like a web. Sometimes people think of the dharmas, as discussed in Abhidharma, as being like separate entities. However, they are not separate. They interact and there is a sense of cohesion. This is why the table has a particular "life" and does not disintegrate. For the duration of its life, the dharmas interact and work in unison so that the table can exist as a table. It is the same thing with the mind.

Using the Abhidharma teachings as a basis, subsequent Buddhist practitioners, in their continued efforts to contemplate what the Buddha taught and while relying on their own meditative experiences, began to speculate in relation to the Abhidharma teachings and their focus on the dharmas. Practitioners began to wonder: "If everything is impermanent and therefore perishable, how can we explain memory? How can we explain karma? How can we say that a person who has performed karmic deeds will be heir to the fruit of those deeds at a later stage in the future? If everything were perishable, the karmic seeds, themselves, would be perishable. How could they persist if everything has only a short life?"

The later practitioners started to think about it on two different levels. One level holds that things as we see them are not "really real" and have only conventional existence rather than ultimate existence, as I mentioned earlier with the example of tables and chairs. A contrary view asserts, however, that the constituent parts of tables actually *do* have existence and that the same applies to time: the past, present, and future. According to this view, time taken as a whole, does not have ultimate existence but, nevertheless, time broken up into time-units does have existence. Therefore, past, present, and future all have what is called *svabhava*, which means "inherent existence." We have to understand this stance because it needs to be distinguished from the Mahayana concept of emptiness.

To make sense of the concept, "emptiness," we have to be familiar with this earlier history because, later, the Mahayanists were critical of this position and spoke instead about emptiness and the lack of svabhava. The earlier group, who posited the existence of phenomena, and spoke of them as being endowed with svabhava or inherent existence—in opposition to the view that phenomena have only conventional existence—gradually formed into a distinct school that came to be known as the "Sarvastivada." Sarvastivada means the "school" or "exponents of the belief that everything exists, who believe in the existence of things, that phenomena have inherent existence." Other schools similar to the Sarvastivada were active at that time, one of which was called the "Pudgalavadins," pudgala meaning "person." Basically, this school claimed that Buddha did not say there is no self but, rather, that there is no soul, which is a different matter. Their claim that the soul does not exist but a person does, is in reference to the five *skandhas*, the five aggregates—form, which denotes physicality or corporeality, feelings, perceptual experiences, dispositional tendencies, and consciousness. The Pudgalavadins said that what we call a "person" cannot be seen to be identical to these constituent parts, nor as completely different. They held the idea that there is something called "personhood," that is neither identical to, nor separate from, the five psychophysical constituents.

Hinayana

These different schools of thought that developed came to be known, collectively, as the "Hinayana" or "small vehicle." When the Mahayana followers came along, they distinguished themselves from Hinayana because they disagreed with them on philosophical points regarding the question of what is actually real, what actually exists, in terms of the ontological status of reality. The Mahayanists felt that some followers of early Buddhism had fallen into the extreme of eternalism because they believed in irreducible particles of physical entities or in the reality of momentary thoughts, mental states, and processes.

We need to distinguish Hinayana from what we might call "early Buddhism proper." Theravada, the tradition practiced in Sri Lanka, Thailand, Myanmar, and so on, is different from what we normally refer to as "Hinayana." Identifying Hinayana with Theravada has caused many problems. There is no real similarity between Theravada and the teachings of the Sarvastivadins or Pudgalavadins, the exponents of the "person" school of thought. Many Theravadins have taken offence when Mahayanists characterize them as followers of Hinayana. We have to be clear on that but also on the other point, that when Mahayana uses the word "Hinayana" it does not necessarily pertain to doctrine but to motivation. In terms of their motivation, a Mahayanist is someone who wants to achieve enlightenment for the sake of others, while a Hinayanist wants to achieve enlightenment for their own benefit and welfare.

Hinayana and Mahayana

Atisha was one of the early Indian masters who went to Tibet. He was from Bengal and was very well travelled, having spent quite a bit of time in Indonesia. Atisha was one of the main teachers to bring the mind-training or lojong[30] practice to Tibet. When he came to Tibet, he established the mind-training school, which came to be known as the "Kadampa." His book, *Lamp on the Bodhisattva Path*, became an established way of describing the aspirants of the dharmic path, and is studied by Tibetans of all four schools—the Gelug, Sakya, Nyingma, and Kagyu. The text describes people of three scopes: those of inferior scope, those of middling scope, and those of superior scope, a system referred to earlier to describe individuals at various stages on the path. In the text, Atisha says that people of inferior scope want to attain enlightenment for themselves, for their own benefit. The people of middling scope also want to work for their own benefit, and it is only the last category, those of superior scope, who want to attain enlightenment for the sake of everyone. We can see therefore, from that description, that only the last group represents Mahayana while the other two represent the Hinayana path. Basically, Atisha's meaning is that even if we learn about Mahayana teachings and take them on board, if our motivation is to attain enlightenment for our own sake and not for the benefit of others, then we are, in fact, following the Hinayana path and not that of Mahayana. What determines whether one is following the Mahayana path or the Hinayana path is one's motivation, what impels us to embark on the path. This is a very helpful way to look at it. On the doctrinal side, the Hinayana schools went into extinction and their unpopularity may have been to do with the radical views they held, which mainstream Buddhists found unpalatable and could not accept. Without a big following, gradually, a school will become weakened over time and this may be what happened to these schools when they disappeared hundreds of years ago.

The basis or the determining factor remains the motivation, irrespective of the tradition one follows. If we are following the

Theravada tradition and we have bodhicitta—even if we do not call it "bodhicitta"—if we want to attain enlightenment for the benefit of others, then we are following Mahayana. If we think we are following Mahayana teachings but our motivation is not that of a Mahayanist, then we are not following Mahayana.

Further, many scholars of the past commented that the Mahayana, even in India, developed completely independently of the early Buddhist monastic institutions. However, in more recent times, upon studying accounts that Chinese pilgrims gave of their visits to India in the early 3rd and 4th centuries, scholars say that the so-called "Mahayana" and "Hinayana" monks lived together in the same monasteries. The councils of that time were called to resolve disputes, not of doctrine, but of Vinaya rules. Certain monks were expelled, not over doctrinal issues, but because they were not following the monastic rules, as laid down in the Vinaya rulebooks. This is important to remember.

Many scholars say that a number of Mahayana sutras may have been written from the 1st century onwards until the 5th or 6th centuries, when the sutras had become popular and well-established. Scholars also suggest that Mahayana may not have been as strong in India as it became in China and subsequently in other parts of East Asia, because Buddhism arrived in China much earlier than it did in Tibet, for instance, in the 1st century. With that in mind, then, certain commentators also say that some of the so-called Sanskrit Mahayana sutras may actually have been written in Central Asia and then translated back into Sanskrit and propagated in India. In any case, what seems certain is that Hinayana and Mahayana monks lived together in the same monasteries and followed the same Vinaya. Even to this day, we follow the same Vinaya and, in fact, as Tibetans, we follow the Vinaya of the Sarvastivada school. The doctrine of the Sarvastivada school died out, but we have preserved and still practice the Vinaya of the

Sarvastivada. These points should be mentioned because in recent years there has been increased tension between the so-called Mahayanists and the Hinayanists—yet it may not be so clear-cut. It may have taken many centuries for Mahayana to develop definable characteristics. Many scholars actually suspect this to be the case.

10

Yogacara

One of the major Mahayana Buddhist schools is known as the "Vijnanavada." The Vijnanavada school is associated with the name, "Cittamatra," which can be translated as "mind only school" (Tib. *sem tsampa*), and is also sometimes identified with the term, "Yogacara." A follower of Vijnanavada could be termed a "mentalist" or "idealist" since vijnana means "mind," and vadin means a "proponent" or "exponent of the mind." This school of thought is often referred to as "Buddhist idealism," but "idealism" in Western philosophy, following George Berkeley, for example, means that everything is seen as solely the individual's own ideas and that there is nothing outside. Berkeley went so far as to say that there is no external world; that when an object is not being perceived, then that object actually does not exist. When critics asked, "What happens when you leave your library or your study? When you are not there, would the books in your study disappear?" "No," he said, "because God is perceiving them." To contrast realism and idealism, "realism" means one believes in a reality that is independent of the mind, and idealists, on the other hand, say that there is no independent reality apart from our mind. So the difference between them is not in reference to a political argument regarding realism versus idealism. Rather, it is about the philosophical idea of what is mental and what is not mental.

Buddhist idealists have made somewhat similar statements, but it is quite different from the British empiricists' variety of idealism. It differs too from Emmanuel Kant's version of idealism since he said that reality is something that exists in itself that we cannot know about. He called reality, *das Ding an sich*, and, in his magnum opus, *A Critique of Pure Reason*, he said that we cannot have knowledge of that. Kant's thinking was that all we can know is what we experience and everything that we experience is dependent upon the mind, due to how the mind employs categorical thought and how we structure our perception of the world.

As was mentioned, the Vijnanavadins are also called "Yogacarins," which means "practitioners of yoga." Their philosophy comes from their meditative practices. This school of thought was initiated by the brothers, Asanga and Vasubhandu. Vasubhandu, the younger brother, was a passionate follower of the Abhidharma teachings and was the author of the classic text on Abhidharma, called *Abhidharmakosha*, which all Tibetan students, including the young monks, have to learn. Nevertheless, his older brother, Asanga, was able to persuade him to become a Vijnanavadin or Yogacarin meditation practitioner. Through meditation then, they realized that everything that we experience is dependent on the mind. In this context, the question arises, "Even if there were mind-independent reality, what would that reality be without mind?" There is no independent way to look at reality. Whatever we think reality is, it can be understood only in relation to the terms and conditions set by the mind that we have: how we are wired to see and experience things. There is no other way; we cannot see in any other way because there is no independent way to look at what is real.

So yoga, in this Yogacara context, means "meditation" and not "Hatha yoga" or even "yoga exercise." Yoga simply means "union" or "bringing opposites together." You meditate, and then you see that everything is dependent on your mind. The Yogacarins said that much of what we experience comes through our senses, but what we experience through our senses does not reflect reality. It is not the case that when we see something, or smell something, or taste something, the information we gather is existing completely independently of our mind. This is because whatever we experience through our senses is processed in relation to our thoughts, emotions, and feelings. It is referred to as the "sixth sense" so, in this context, even the mind is regarded as a sense.

In addition to that, we have what is called the "egoic mind." We personalize everything that we experience. It is not just that we see something and leave it at that, but we unconsciously think, "I experienced this." "I saw this." "I smelt that." "I heard that." "I touched this." It is appropriated in such a way that one claims some kind of ownership of what one experiences. "It is my experience!" Of course, one is not consciously saying to oneself, "I saw a car. Oh, that is my experience," but nevertheless, we unconsciously think, "I saw a car." If we happen to remember, later on, when somebody asks if we saw a car, we say, "Yes, I saw that red car." While we are driving along the road, as we take all these sensory impressions in, we process this, unconsciously saying to ourselves, "I am experiencing this. I am experiencing it." We always relate it back to ourselves. So this is the egoic mind, in Yogacarin thought. We claim some kind of ownership and say, "It's me. I experienced that."

The Yogacarins say that when we do this, the impressions created in the mind do not simply persist for a while and then disappear. It is not like blowing on a mirror and then after a short period of time the condensation disappears without leaving a trace. Yogacarin thought says it is not like that. Rather, we store information in our unconscious, in what is called the "storehouse consciousness" (Skt. *alayavijnana*; Tib. *kunzhi namshe*). *Alaya* means the "basis" and *vijnana* is "consciousness." All that we experience leaves an impression in the mind and it remains dormant until we are confronted with other similar stimuli. It is then that the dormant traces and dispositions in the alayavijnana are stimulated or awakened. This is why we see things that are different from each other as being the same, why there is no change. Due to accumulated traces and dispositions, we may see something different, but we do not recognize the difference and, instead, see the similarities. Change, then, is difficult. It is very difficult for us to change because we do not see change. We see sameness. Even if things have changed, we do not see the change. We think the same thing is happening, that it is a recurring thing when, in fact, it is not. This is what Yogacarins or Vijnanavadins say and it is very important to remember this. This is how our karmic patterns, karmic cause and effect as it applies to us, is perpetuated, and the imprints in our mind are responsible.

This is what the Yogacarins say about the mind. They say it is because of this that we have to think about reality in three different ways. First, there is what is termed "ultimate reality"; then the concept of relative reality; and finally, the reality of ideation, which refers to a reality based on our own thoughts and ideas. The Yogacarins say that we have to think about reality in terms of degrees—that is, in relation to how much of the reality we perceive is dependent upon our minds, and whether what we perceive is completely mind-created, mind-dependent, or not dependent on the mind at all. Buddhist idealism does not say, "There is no reality apart from our mind," as many people have claimed, in relation to Asanga and Vasubandhu's school of thought. Buddhist idealists do not say that everything is the mind, that there is no reality apart from the mind. In relation to ultimate reality, what they say is that, ultimately, there is no difference between reality and the mind, that the reality which exists is not separate from the mind, so, far from saying, "It is all mind," they say that whatever ultimately exists is not separate from the mind.

Following this, the Yogacarins speak of relative reality, which has to do with the interaction or interface between the perceiver and the perceived (Skt. *grahya* and *grahaka*; Tib. *zungzin*). For example, we perceive something, we see something, we smell something, we taste or touch something. We also think about abstract ideas, like justice, human rights, and so on, which are examples of dependent reality (Tib. *kuntak zhenwang yongdrup*). This has to do with cause and effect, and with subject and object. It also relates to binary concepts—for example, the perceiver and the perceived; morality: what is right and what is wrong, and so on. It is easy to see the framework of binary concepts operating within the area of morality when we observe that what is right is only right because there is something called "wrong" and what is wrong is only wrong because there is something called "right" and so on. So these are also dependent on the mind.

There is another kind of reality that is based on what we might call "phantasmagoria." We think of a unicorn, but there is no unicorn, yet it has some reality. It has reality to the extent that we can think of such a creature, even though that creature does not exist. This is the completely "made-up mind," a mind of pure imagination. So this is why the Yogacarins say that we have to think about reality in degrees, in terms of how much of the reality is dependent on the mind. Whatever we have simply made up in our heads has no reality at all, apart from the fact that it is in our heads. Beyond that level, other things have more reality because they are dependent upon how we conceptualize them, categorize them, pigeonhole things, and even how we use language and concepts— for example, species and genera. We want to put things in neat pigeonholes so that we are able to make some sense of them.

Then we have the ideally absolute, the absolute reality. For the Yogacarins or Vijnanavadins, because they are Mahayanists, what is absolutely real is emptiness. Emptiness and the mind itself, the nature of the mind, are not different. Emptiness is not the same as non-existence; non-existence is the opposite of existence, so emptiness is not the opposite of existence. We have to understand this. Emptiness and existence go together. According to the Mahayana way of thinking, nothing can exist if there is no emptiness. Things exist because of emptiness, so to think that emptiness has something to do with non-existence is to fall into what the Mahayanists call the "nihilistic extreme." When we talk about the non-existence of something, that means one thinks it does not exist; therefore, it is the opposite of existence. Emptiness, then, is not the opposite of existence. Things exist, as Nagarjuna said, *because* of emptiness. Because things have an empty nature, therefore everything will be possible.

11
Madhyamaka

This takes us to the other Mahayana view, the philosophical school of thought called "Madhyamaka." Madhyamaka means the "Middle Way school" or the "Middle View school." The Middle Way school says that in regard to existence and non-existence, thinking in a binary, dualistic way prevents us from seeing things properly. It is very important in Buddhism to learn to see things in a different way. Nagarjuna, the founder of Madhyamaka, said that to understand emptiness, first we should think about cause and effect. Instead of looking at things in an isolated way, we should be looking at how they interact, how they influence each another, how the body and mind, for example, impact on each other, how our self-perception impacts on our physical health, and how our physical ill-health impacts on our mental state.

When we start to see it that way, we are looking in terms of relationship. We are paying more attention to the relationships between things, rather than isolating them, which is what we normally do. We just wrest things out of context and then we become focused on that. We think, "This is what is going on, this is what is happening" and the context, the relationship—everything, is forgotten. Whatever we may think is going on becomes isolated, wrested from its context, and so we get a completely distorted view of what is happening. However, if we pay attention to the relationship between things, we get a much wider, more comprehensive way of understanding what is really happening because, as Buddhism says, there is a ripple effect going on. The world is not static and inert. To put it simply, even with what we think of as physical substances, there is a state of dynamism. There is always something going on. This is why a table may fall apart, but it does not happen overnight because there is dynamism. There are always things happening. All the internal elements that constitute a table are interacting with each other. Then, at some stage, decay will occur.

Nagarjuna, as founder of the Madhyamaka school of thought, is even taken seriously by Western philosophers. They think he was one of the most sophisticated thinkers of philosophy, but what he had to say is actually not so difficult to understand. He said that to understand emptiness, you need to look at relationships, and when you look at relationships, then you can see that there are always at least two related things in a given context. Often, if we look at two things that are related to each other, then we find that those two things are also related to further things. If we look at ourselves and then at our parents, and then at our parents' siblings—as in a family tree, for example—the same kinds of relationships are happening. In every life experience we have, the same kinds of relationships go on.

Paying attention to that will allow us to see what reality is, and that will allow us to understand what emptiness means. As Nagarjuna said, emptiness does not mean non-existence. He said that emptiness means seeing things as not having self-sufficiency. Nothing has self-sufficient existence (Skt. *svabhava*). When we have *samskara*,[31] for example, it causes us to think in a dichotomous way, so we do not see relationships but, instead, want to separate things. Our conceptual mind works in that way; we separate things because we want to be clear. We want to see what is different.

This, of course, has its uses. I am not saying that Mahayana

Buddhists deny that it is a useful thing to do but, when we separate things, because we are so habituated, we do not see the relationship. We do not see what gives rise to what and we do not see the causal nexus, the causal relationships that exist among many different things. We may think that it is only directly related matters that would have causal impact on each other, but there may be other elements not directly related to a particular aspect, whatever it is, that are still impacted by what is going on. There is that ripple effect, in other words. This is what Nagarjuna said. *Asvabhava*, or lack of inherent existence, is emptiness so emptiness does not mean "non-existence." As Nagarjuna cautioned, "If you think like that, then it is like holding a venomous snake incorrectly: you are bitten and injected with lethal poison." If we think of emptiness as non-existent, as nothingness, then we fall into the pitfall of nihilism. Nagarjuna added that it is like holding a snake by the wrong end—which I'm sure means you try to grab the snake by the throat. Of course, if we grabbed the snake by the tail, and held it away from us, then it is said the snake could not bite us.

So we do not think of emptiness as nothingness; we think of emptiness as dependent arising (Skt. *pratityasamutpada*; Tib. *tenching drelwar jungwa*). Everything is dependently arising because if things were not in relationship, nothing could arise; everything would be inert, and nothing would happen. Nagarjuna says that even life itself would be impossible. We would not be able to breathe. There would be no organisms; there would be nothing. The world would be completely desolate and nothing at all would be happening. But things do happen and life exists because of all the causes and conditions that are present. When causes and conditions come together, then things happen, and if these causes and conditions begin to separate, diminish, or disappear, then whatever it is that sustained that particular life would also come to an end.

If we looked at it that way, Nagarjuna says, we would not get so upset, depressed, or so greedy and needy. If something has not worked out very well, we need not think that this is the end of us, that everything is finished—rather, because of interdependent arising, we can create the kinds of causes and conditions that might bring about what we want to have in our lives. We do not have to leave it up to the universe for things to happen. We are also players, participants, in the whole drama. Due to the idea of interaction, as I was saying earlier, and because of the relationship that exists between varieties of elements, if we do our bit and do it properly, then we can also make things happen. So we do not have to think, "Things were really good for a while and now it has all gone and I am depressed and lonely, a nothing, a nobody." Nagarjuna advises that his philosophy has to be translated into daily life so that we begin to see things differently and, by seeing things differently, we will act differently. It is to be used like a therapy that will help our mental disturbances.

Such an approach is needed because, as Nagarjuna explains, when we are not looking at relationships, we get fixated on certain events, situations, or people, and everything else fades into the background. That one issue we are obsessed about becomes very prominent, we fixate on that, and all the undesirable emotions well up in our mind. If we do not do that, but see things in context, the anger or jealousy, or whatever emotion it is, will start to diminish. Even if it did not disappear altogether, it would at least diminish. The hold these things have over us will diminish, and our quality of life, as a consequence, will improve. We spend far too much time worrying about varieties of things. Worries, anxieties, powerful negative emotions, and even mood disturbances can follow from fixation. When we have strong negative emotions, the mood disturbances follow naturally. When we worry, we get anxious and depressed—that is the natural consequence, because we are telling ourselves the wrong story. I will address this again in the section on psychology.

Fixation

Fixation (Tib. *dzinpa*), causes mental disturbances because nothing, apart from what one is fixated and focused on, is considered important. We should not allow ourselves to get to that level. One of the most effective antidotes for this is to try to put the situation in context by seeing it in terms of relationship, recognizing it as having happened because of causes and conditions. We try not to blame ourselves entirely, or the other person, although that does not mean that one of those involved should not be blamed if something unethical has happened, let us say, in terms of human relationships. In Buddhism, when somebody must take responsibility for something, we take that very seriously because we believe in karma. However, even with karma, you would see that in context, so you may think, "I didn't want to do it, but I did it, and under the circumstances I felt pressured" or "I was very angry" or "I was in a delusional state." If we see ourselves in that context, then a lot of the solidity attached to strong emotions begins to diminish. This is what Nagarjuna and others have said. In reality, even these strong emotions do not have svabhava or inherent existence because emotions arise due to causes and conditions. The Mahayanists say that emotions arise like clouds in the sky. The clouds are there because of causes and conditions and, when the causes and conditions are not there, the clouds disappear.

12

Madhyamaka, Emptiness, and Compassion

Mahayanists were critical of some of the interpreters of Abhidharma teachings and Nagarjuna was one of the first central Mahayana teachers to take this up. Nagarjuna was following Mahayana sutras such as *Prajnaparamita Sutra*, which speak about emptiness, to attack the idea presented in some Abhidharma commentaries that phenomena have svabhava. In Buddhist philosophy, in order to criticize someone else's position, we rely on two things: *lung rikpa* in Tibetan. *Lung* means "textual authority" and *rikpa* means "reasoning" or "logic." Nagarjuna relied upon both. He used the prajnaparamita literature for textual authority, saying that interpreters of Abhidharma make assertions that contradict what prajnaparamita is saying. He also attacked the position of the Abhidharma interpreters, based on logical inconsistencies, explaining that it does not make sense to say that things have inherent existence because nothing can exist of its own accord. When we say that something exists, it is understood that it exists only on a provisional level, in a manner of speaking. If, however, the word "exists" is meant to convey that something has independent existence, Nagarjuna said there is no such thing. There is nothing that exists by itself, of its own accord, because everything is dependent on something else.

In relation to emptiness, in Buddhism the word "essence" is used as a technical term. "Essence" refers to a substance that does not depend on anything other than itself. According to Madhyamaka, there is no such substance, the reason being that everything that exists, every substance, is dependent on something else. Therefore, when we say "empty" or "emptiness," this actually means "empty of inherent existence," or "empty of a self-sufficiently existing substance." If we have some appreciation of this idea, we will realize that Buddhism does not say that everything is empty and so therefore everything is unreal. This is why in Buddhism, Madhyamaka posits the two-tier theory of truth, which is relative or conventional truth, and ultimate truth.

With conventional truth, a distinction is made between conventional truth that is illusory, and conventional truth that is veridical. If conventional or relative truth were nothing but illusory, they would not have used the word "truth" in the name. If that were the case, then nothing about conventional truth could be true so why would the word "truth" be used? Secondly, why make the distinction between conventional truth which is illusory, and conventional truth which is non-illusory?

In making this distinction, Nagarjuna and other founders of this school of thought, used the example of a rope and a snake. If one is walking down a dark alleyway and the visibility is poor, one may think one sees a snake but, instead, it is actually a striped rope. Seeing the rope as a snake is conventionally illusory; but the fact that the rope is there is conventionally veridical. It is there. It is real. In that way, we should not think that conventional truth is completely illusory. This would be a mistake.

Madhyamaka philosophers like Chandrakirti and so on, have said that if conventional truth had no reality whatsoever, there would be no point in embarking on the Buddhist path, doing meditation, doing good works, or aspiring to become liberated from the bondage and misery that is samsara. There would be no point at all. All these activities are important because, on the conventional level, they are true. The ultimate truth is not found separately or independently of the conventional truth. For this reason also, conventional truth is real because ultimate truth is the *nature* of conventional truth. The nature of conventional truth is not to be found anywhere else.

Nagarjuna further extended the concept of interdependent origination and this can be seen in his statement that if you understood emptiness, you would understand interdependent origination and if you understand interdependent origination you will understand emptiness. Basically, as I mentioned earlier, he said, with this in mind, it cannot mean that nothing exists. Emptiness does not mean things do not have existence. What it means is that things do not have *inherent* existence or svabhava. Such a situation does not exist. When we try to understand Nagarjuna, when we try to understand emptiness, we have to think of the interpreters of Abhidharma to fully appreciate what is being said. When Nagarjuna says things do not have inherent existence, what he is referring to is that things do not have inherent existence in the way that the Sarvastivadins, for example, had been talking about it. When Nagarjuna says things do not exist inherently, we should think of the Sarvastivadin position and their claim that things have inherent existence, that things have svabhava.

Interdependent Arising and Compassion

Nagarjuna thought that because things are interdependently produced, if we understand interdependent arising, we will then develop wisdom and that if we develop genuine wisdom, then compassion will arise. His idea was that if we think of things as interdependently arising, even in terms of emotions and feelings, we will have a better sense of how we exist, how we live in the world, and how we interact with others. Then we will not be thinking, "I have this ego or self which stands alone, which stands aloof, and is untethered, independent, like a solitary entity." We will then understand that our sense of selfhood is dependent on others and on our own self-perception, our perception of ourselves. It is mutually conditioned. He says that self and other are mutually conditioning concepts. His basic point is that we cannot have something called sense of self without thinking of other selves, in relation to one's own self, and vice versa.

In this way, from an understanding of interdependent arising, we can see that from emptiness, compassion may arise. This is quite important. Some scholars have found the idea of emptiness or insubstantiality to be incompatible with compassion, and examples of this academic dilemma can be found.[32] When we understand interdependent arising and emptiness, because we are not so fixated on our self, or fixated on the idea that the self has inherent existence, then we become more open to others. We become more open to the world at large. Compassion then arises naturally. As is often quoted in Mahayana teachings, "The essence of emptiness is compassion." *Tongnyi nyingjé nyingpo chen*, means "emptiness is the essence of compassion." Our lack of compassion and real feeling, our stunted feelings and emotions, come about because of our egoic preoccupation. Our egoic preoccupation is based on a misunderstanding of ourselves: we think that there is something in us, an agent, that stands by itself. Nagarjuna tries to show that this is not the case. He maintains that for an agent to be an agent, it must have the capacity to perform the action and there needs to be an object of the action. Now if we take an agent and their action, Nagarjuna says, often we may think that the agent has primacy over actions, that actions are performed by the agent, and that the agent is more real. We think that without an agent there would be no actions performed, but this is not true, according to Nagarjuna. Agent and action mutually define each other. An "agent" that does not perform actions is not an agent. An agent is an agent only because actions are performed. They have equal status. In addition, the action performed would not realize its full potential if there were no object upon which the action had been performed so there has to be an object as well. There is the agent, there is the action, and there is the object of one's action and these have to come together. If we see it like that, Nagarjuna says, we will understand emptiness, we will see asvabhava. We will see asvabhava, or lack of svabhava of the agent, lack of svabhava of the action, and lack of svabhava of the object, because they are mutually dependent on each other. Again, action is something that is interdependently produced.

Middle View

To revisit Nagarjuna's argument, he tries to arrive at the middle way, what he calls the "Middle View." He says the Middle View avoids the extremes of nihilism and eternalism and that he is not teaching nonexistence of phenomena but the nonexistence of inherent phenomena: non-inherent existence of the agent, non-inherent existence of the action, and non-inherent existence of the object of the action. Nagarjuna says the same about emotions and feelings: that none of these has svabhava. Emotions are brought about by causes and conditions: subject, object, emotions, feelings, or whatever the case might be. He says if we see things that way, then we will see emptiness and will arrive at the Middle View. If, however, we fail to do that, he says that it is actually better to believe that we have a self or ego, rather than thinking there is no self or ego. Nagarjuna makes this comment in his magnum opus called *Mulamadhyamakakarika*, which means "Root Insight of the Middle Way." A basic translation of *Mulamadhyamakakarika* would be: *karika* means "texts," *mula* means "root," and Madhyamaka is the Middle Way.

When Nagarjuna says we should try to grasp the idea of emptiness but that, if we have doubts, it is better to believe that things have svabhava—his explanation is that if we think they do not have any reality at all then everything will collapse. He points out that then we would have no values, no social decorum, and no moral compass. It would be a case of "anything goes" and then everything would be chaos. Nagarjuna then reminds us that emptiness is not like that. He says that trying to understand emptiness will help us, whereas, on the other hand, thinking that things have svabhava will fuel the flame of craving and grasping.

Emptiness is the antidote that will curb craving. It will help us reduce our suffering. Nagarjuna talks about suffering in this way. He says that even with the idea of suffering and the cause of suffering, we should be thinking along these lines: that suffering comes about due to causes and conditions and those causes and conditions themselves are dependent upon further causes and conditions. He says if we look at it like that, it defuses the whole thing. Normally, due to our myopia, we zoom in. We just pick out certain features in our field of experience and become fixated on them and everything else is discarded and paid no attention to. If we see how things are interconnected, then we will know how they work, how they operate, and because of this, it will defuse the situation. For example, if we decide that something or other is the cause of our problems and have singled out a particular incident or individual, Nagarjuna counsels us to look at that in relation to causes and conditions and then we will be able to see other factors which may have contributed to whatever has come to pass. It defuses our fixation and that will automatically help us. When we become fixated on something and it gets into our head—colloquially speaking, when we get "a bee in our bonnet" about something—then whatever we latch onto will become more and more real. The degree of reality of whatever we have fixated on in our experience becomes greater and greater. The more tenaciously we latch onto something, the more real it becomes. Nagarjuna's point, again, is that if we try to look at the interconnected causes and conditions that are present in a situation, our fixation will be defused. Then, if our fixation is defused, our tendency to cling to and grasp at things, and our fixation, will be loosened. So according to Nagarjuna, that is how emptiness can help.

Nagarjuna likens emptiness to a medicine, in a similar way to the Buddha referring to the Dharma as medicine. By understanding emptiness, our suffering will become lessened, not because we do not care any longer, but because we realize that caring about things and fixation do not go together properly. As far as Nagarjuna was concerned, we care in a much more authentic fashion when we are not so obsessed, not so fixated on certain things and, gradually, we will be able to develop a caring attitude towards varieties of things. In our confused state, we are prejudiced and biased in the way we interact with others and live in the world. We are partial to certain things; we favor particular things. Nagarjuna says that it is the wrong way to think if we believe that we will not be able to have deep feelings or be a caring person, as a result of thinking about the emptiness of things and of one's being, thinking that everything is emptiness.

Actually, it is quite the contrary. If we no longer get so obsessed, so fixated, then we begin to care more because we are working with our fixation. We become less prejudiced, less biased, and begin to see things with a much broader, more expansive view. An expansive view is what we do not have at the moment. We have a very narrow view, but if our approach is in terms of the interconnectedness of all things and seeing things as not having inherent existence, then we will have the expansive view.

Bodhicitta and Becoming a Bodhisattva

With the expansive view comes expansive bodhicitta, to use the Mahayana expression. Bodhicitta means "enlightened heart." The enlightened heart responds to all kinds of phenomena, experiences, and situations in a less biased and more caring fashion than the way we are used to. We may care about animals, but not care so much about human beings. We have all kinds of issues like that. We may care about people dying in some African nation or in India but, if somebody is dying in our street, we may just walk past them.

Nagarjuna's point is that bodhicitta will arise if we have a more sensitized perspective and, if that happens, one is becoming a bodhisattva. This is what Mahayana Buddhism says. In Mahayana, one tries to become a bodhisattva. Through understanding all of these things, one may become a bodhisattva. People read Mahayana texts like the Flower Garden Sutra (Skt. *Avatamsakasutra*), and the Lotus Sutra (Skt. *Saddhara Pundarika Sutra*), and in these sutras they observe bodhisattvas performing heroic deeds and sacrificial acts, such as plucking out their eyes and giving them to a blind person, and other amazing and sometimes macabre things. Some of these people might think that such teachings are actually telling us that if we want to become a bodhisattva, then we should literally perform actions like this. In fact, there are two different categories of sutra. One type of sutra is there to give us inspiration and these teachings are called "interpretive teachings" (Skt. *neyartha*), which means they are not to be taken literally. In Buddhism, in reality, we do not do harm to ourselves or to others so killing oneself for a greater cause, martyring oneself, is not seen as acceptable or virtuous behavior. Sometimes edifying stories are told, which are like a cosmic play, with heroes and villains.

Buddhist teachings are said to be very skillful and work on many different aspects of us. Even with our mind, the Dharma works on many different levels: on the feeling level, the imagination level, and on the intellect. Sutras such as the *Prajnaparamita Sutra*, contain the other category of teachings, the definitive teachings (Skt. *nitartha*). Nitartha means "definitive." We do not need to interpret, or wonder what the sutra means. When the sutra says that things are empty, we do not need to ask what that means.

Teachings on emptiness are not symbolic but definitive. They do not need to be interpreted.

The interpretive teachings that we spoke of earlier, the teachings that need to be interpreted are there to arouse certain emotions and feelings that, unlike our normal emotions, are beneficial emotions. We become inspired, moved in a positive way. According to Buddhism, when this happens, we actually accumulate merit. We read inspiring stories, which may bring tears to our eyes. We might read the sutra of the "ever-weeping" bodhisattva. This bodhisattva is a crybaby, so when some little thing happens, he is overcome. We might read that sutra and be overcome ourselves and start getting all teary-eyed—but if we do, this is good. It is much better than watching some soap opera and getting teary-eyed. We read these stories and we are moved and inspired, and that is the purpose. There are many teachings like this; again, they are the interpretive teachings or neyartha teachings. We have to understand it like that.

The other point is that when we become a bodhisattva, it does not mean that we actually have to be the same as the bodhisattvas described in the literature. We need to think of the bodhisattva path as being just that, a path. It has a beginning and an end, however, the point of the whole exercise is not to think of the end but of the beginning and the middle. The idea is that if we do not think about our own enlightenment but do whatever is needed to benefit ourselves and others with the understanding we have about interdependent arising, emptiness, and so on, then we will stay on course and enlightenment is assured. Even though "three karmic eons" are mentioned, it does not mean it will literally take three karmic eons. The idea is to have courage and fortitude. In the Mahayana literature, Shantideva and others like him point out that it is very important to have fortitude and courage. We should try not to think, "I have to escape this samsaric prison as fast as I can," but, rather, think, "With proper understanding, I will see samsara and nirvana as not being completely separate."

Samsara is not something to leave behind and nirvana something that we try to rush to. Through greater understanding of the world that surrounds us, then something of the nirvanic vision can be realized. Trying to bring that vision to others and also develop that within oneself is the idea. The term, "three countless eons," is just thrown in so that you think it could take forever. After all: "countless"—how do you count something that is countless? And three times over? It baffles your mind. In that way, we think of emptiness as being inseparable from wisdom mind. If we looked at it like this, thinking that emptiness is not separate from true, authentic compassion, then we could not fall into the nihilistic trap and we would see everything as empty in relation to wisdom mind, and from the wisdom mind would issue genuine compassion. As it says in Mahayana Buddhism, as Mahayana practitioners, we should lay the seeds for realization of Buddha's physical body and for realization of his mental body. The physical body is called "rupakaya" and the mental body is called "arupakaya" or "non-physical body."

Rupakaya or physical body is attained through compassionate activity. Rather than being merely a vague description, the term "compassionate activity" refers to concrete actions like being generous, extending ourselves to others, and following moral precepts—which means not lying or cheating or taking life, and so on. We have to be patient, which means not just wanting to get quick results, but thinking about doing the things that need to be done. To think that what needed to be done is done—that is the reward; one has already obtained the reward for one's actions. This is true, yet we think that "action" is one thing and "reward" is something else. Vigor—which means, "not relenting," "being persistent in a proper manner," and "not giving up" is also seen as a virtuous quality. Therefore, generosity, moral precepts, patience, and vigor are examples of "compassionate activity," and this activity can be practiced with a greater or lesser level of depth.

With compassion, generally, it is said that first we develop compassion towards living beings (Tib. *semchen la mikpay nyingjé*). We generate compassion for all living beings so the intentional object of our compassion is all living beings. The second one is called the "compassion that takes all things, everything, as the object of compassion" (Tib. *chö la mikpay nyingjé*). The last one is called "compassion without object" (Tib. *mikpa mepay nyingjé*).

Chö la mikpay means "taking all dharmas as objects of compassion" so this includes our biosphere and everything that exists. Objectless compassion means "compassion imbued with a sense of emptiness," so there is no division between the object of compassion, the experience of compassion, and the subject who is experiencing compassion. There is no object; it is self-radiating compassion. It radiates in all directions but is not aimed in any direction by an agent. There are three levels. All three levels are necessary to have compassion, but objectless compassion is the subtlest and most advanced, while compassion directed towards living beings is the most basic and necessary. Based on that, one develops the other two forms of compassion. In Mahayana Buddhism, that is how compassion is spoken of. There are many other ways to describe compassion so it is helpful to learn what Mahayana Buddhism says about it and not just assume we know what is meant when compassion is spoken of. Mahayana Buddhism has specific ways of describing compassion, which include how to develop and understand compassion, and these are important. If we do that, then we will become a bodhisattva.

In Mahayana Buddhism, there is a devotional aspect as well, which I think we need to mention. The notion of trust, being able to place our trust in a greater being, is taken seriously. We are being helped along the way by the buddhas and bodhisattvas, so we may appeal to Avalokiteshvara, Tara, or Manjushri, and so on.[33] This is seen as a way of making us feel uplifted, so when we feel discouraged, when we feel a little weary, the idea is that we should invoke the bodhisattvas. When we do that, we feel that they have come to our aid, that some help is at hand, that we are not alone and left to our own devices. We feel that we are transported to another level. Chanting and invoking the names of buddhas and bodhisattvas is also important and very much a part of Mahayana Buddhist practice. We can invoke the names of particular bodhisattvas who represent a specific quality for whatever we may need. If we are ill and need healing or even if we need to pass an exam, we may want to invoke the name of Manjushri. The devotional aspect of Mahayana practices is as important as the other aspects and, again, this is thought of in relation to wisdom and compassion, because all the buddhas and bodhisattvas represent these two qualities and manifest them in their unique ways.

13

Mahayana, Bodhicitta, and Six Paramitas

As mentioned in the previous chapter, when we embark on the Mahayana path, we need to be supported by the two principal practices of Mahayana: the cultivation of wisdom and the practice of compassion. These two are indispensable. Without them, we cannot practice Mahayana. If, in addition to following the Mahayana path, we also wish to follow the bodhisattva path of Mahayana, it does not mean that we have to be perfect or flawless. As Shantideva says, we can generate bodhicitta or enlightened heart in two different ways. At the beginning, we should develop the intention to work as a bodhisattva to benefit others. Even if one achieves only that, one has taken a giant step forward. We should not think, "What is the point of thinking about doing something beneficial but not actually getting to do it, not getting to do anything concrete that has practical benefits for ourselves and others?"

Shantideva says it is not like that; it is like planting seeds in one's mind. It is similar to having a desire to take a journey somewhere—say, to India. The more one thinks of it, the more chance there is of actually undertaking the journey. So, if one has the desire to embark on the bodhisattva path and do something beneficial, one has already generated bodhicitta, and in a sense, has already become a bodhisattva. Even if we have only the desire to benefit others, that is a good thing, but then we may actually decide to take the journey.

Once we begin on the path, however, because we are new, we are bound to make mistakes. Of course, we can take the bodhisattva vow again to reinforce our commitment and that is different from the vows of a monk or nun where if you break the vows, then you cannot really take them back. If you feel you need to reinforce the bodhisattva vow, however, because you think you have backslid or that there have been lapses, then you can renew your commitment. You can restore your original bodhisattva vows. This, in itself, suggests that simply because one has embarked on the bodhisattva path, one is then not expected to be like one of the perfect bodhisattvas, as portrayed in the Buddhist sutras.

There are books on Mahayana, written by Western Buddhist teachers, which basically say that the bodhisattva ideal is simply that, an ideal, and that we cannot expect to become bodhisattvas. They say the way it is described in the texts and sutras is just beyond anyone's reach and not humanly possible. However, it is a big mistake to see it like this. In some sutras, the bodhisattvas are described in very glowing terms, but there are many different kinds of bodhisattvas. Just like human beings, generally, some are very advanced and others are not; there are bodhisattvas who are novices, and bodhisattvas who have gone a long way. It is good to keep that in mind because there has been a series of books with the same kind of theme. They all make the same point, which is that you cannot expect to become a buddha or bodhisattva. They argue that we are human beings and we cannot be perfect, and since we cannot possibly become perfect, then why try? They say trying to be perfect is self-defeating and we should not practice Buddhism with that kind of attitude. Obviously, that is not the traditional view and of course, it is wrong to think like that. As I said, we have to have ideals and we aspire to achieve these.

Six Paramitas

I alluded earlier to the practice of the paramitas or six

transcendental actions, in terms of the development of compassion, generosity, moral precepts, patience, vigor, meditative concentration, and wisdom, which suggests that we actually have to practice. If we were perfect, then we would not have to practice. The paramitas are also called the "six perfections" but not because by doing them we are doing something perfect. Rather, due to the orientation of these practices, they guide us towards perfection, towards the attainment of buddhahood. I will briefly mention the six transcendental actions because, according to Mahayana Buddhism, the practice of compassion is very profound. It is not simply about having sympathetic feelings for the suffering of others, even though that is an essential quality of compassion. In Buddhism, compassion is defined as wanting others to be free of suffering and the causes of suffering. Love, which is often paired with compassion, is described or defined as wanting the causes and conditions to be present for others to have happiness so wishing that others have the causes and conditions of happiness is to have love for others. Wishing that others are free of the causes of suffering is compassion, but that has to be practiced in relation to the six transcendental actions, which I will now briefly discuss.

The practice of generosity has several levels. The first level is material generosity (Skt. *dana*), which means that we give to others. Dana means "giving" or "generosity." The second level is giving protection, which is superior to material gifts, and the third is giving spiritual counseling. Trying to change somebody's attitude towards life in a profound and beneficial way is the best gift that one can give to another person.

The practice of moral precepts (Skt. *shila*) also has three different levels. The first one has to do with practicing morality in terms of restraint. Instead of immediately trying to do something positive, one begins by trying to prevent oneself from doing anything harmful. Even though one may not yet be able to perform a positive act, if one does nothing harmful by having been able to exercise restraint, then that is a good start. That is the fundamental principle of shila. The second one has to do with the gathering of virtuous thoughts, which means that it comes about through practice. When we try to practice mindfulness, for example, we do not just observe things as they come and go, as some people do but, as we do this, we try to get some sense of the sorts of actions that are helpful and of which things are unhelpful or harmful. We then learn to utilize that which is helpful and conducive to one's growth, while developing the qualities we need that have not arisen yet. We need to encourage the qualities already manifest to grow and flourish and if certain qualities that we need are not yet present, we try to make them come into existence. So doing this is called "the gathering of virtuous thoughts," and it relates not just to thoughts, but to emotions and feelings as well. The third level is seen as a particularly bodhisattva-oriented way of practicing shila. In Tibetan, this is called *semchen donje kyi tsultrim*, which means the "shila of benefiting other sentient beings." Not only is one trying not to harm others and developing certain helpful qualities, but one actually engages in concrete actions to benefit others—through generosity, through patience, through vigor, and so on. This is shila paramita.

Following this we have the paramita of patience (Skt. *kshanti*; Tib. *zopa*). There are three different kinds of kshanti as well. The first one is the patience exercised in terms of not being overwhelmed by the obstacles we may encounter in life when we try to work towards achieving a particular goal. That is the first one: not to be overwhelmed by potential obstacles. The second one is called *dukngal dang lengyi zöpa* in Tibetan, which refers to any kind of suffering or hardship. We do not shy away from hardship. When things start to get a little uncomfortable, we should not lose heart and give up, but should see hardship as a form of challenge, as something to work with and to learn and benefit from. In Mahayana teachings, even hardship can be a teacher; we can learn from hardship. The third form of patience is having the patience to understand dharmas. This understanding actually relates to the dharmas as in "things" or mental and physical phenomena, as we have discussed in previous chapters. By doing so, by understanding these, we are trying to understand the Dharma, as in the teachings. Through trying to understand the Dharma we can learn to understand other things. It is exercising patience in that regard.

Then we have the paramita of vigor (Skt. *virya*). This is sometimes translated as "effort," but "effort" seems to imply that we have to exert ourselves or try very hard. In this context, it seems more appropriate to translate virya as "vigor" rather than "effort" because, as Shantideva says, virya has to be understood as having an energizing quality. The first level relates to the idea that when we have vigor, we do not find things difficult. Difficult things actually become easier when we have vigor and feel energetic. When we feel energetic and not wasted and exhausted, then we have the energy to deal with things. It is a good quality to have. The second level is the vigor that comes from enjoying doing what we should be doing. Shantideva has said that this is something we can learn. There is nothing we do that we cannot teach ourselves to enjoy. When we start to enjoy things that we should actually be doing, then it becomes effortless. This is another form of vigor. The third one, again, is about being energetic, being vigorous, in relation to helping others; engaging with others and not staying aloof by cutting off one's connection to other beings.

Following this, we have the paramita of meditative concentration. In order to perform all these activities, one has to practice meditative concentration and use wisdom, as I discussed previously. Wisdom and compassion are seen in that way as the two wings of bodhicitta. The word "bodhicitta," in itself, represents that. *Bodhi* means "awakened," representing wisdom-mind; and *citta* means "heart," so it is the "compassionate heart." Wisdom and compassion are often compared to a lame person and a blind person. If someone who cannot walk but has sight and someone who cannot see but is able to walk come together, the one without sight can carry the one who cannot walk, who, being sighted, will be able to direct their progress. The basic point is that compassion without wisdom is blind, and wisdom without compassion is lame. Nothing can be achieved. You need both.

The Integral Approach to Philosophy

We have been discussing how important the integral approach to philosophy is within Buddhism. With regard to the different philosophical perspectives on reality that we find in Mahayana Buddhist literature, from the integral point of view we do not have to think that Abhidharma and the Yogacarins have it wrong and that only the Madhyamakans have got it right. In Buddhism, the various philosophical schools of thought are not treated equally but are hierarchically organized. I spoke about Abhidharma earlier so, if we follow the hierarchical model and include the Abhidharmists, they are at rock bottom, then come the Yogacarins or idealists, and the Madhyamakans are at the top, with Nagarjuna being seen as the most important figure in Mahayana Buddhism. The key point I want to emphasize is that the three perspectives, Abhidharma, Yogacara, and Madhyamaka, should be integrated. There is no conflict between these schools of thought if we see them in the right way. Why is that the case? It is because, for instance, we can use the Abhidharma theory of dharmas, seeing our thoughts and emotions, each one of them, and isolating them. We can first isolate them and then see the relationships. We may think there is some kind of contradiction but with the integral approach there is no contradiction. For example, when we meditate, we isolate our thoughts: "I am thinking this thing." "Now I am feeling hot." "Now

I am feeling cold." It is actually good to separate things first, thinking that, "I have this thought, this emotion, this feeling," and identify the thought and acknowledge that. It is very important to think like this.

All of these philosophical standpoints can be integrated. There is no reason to think, if we subscribe to the idea of emptiness (Skt. *shunyata*) that we cannot say the mind has supremacy over what we perceive about the world through our senses, or that whatever we perceive through the senses, as processed and organized by the mind, consists of dharmas, the different entities. This would be adopting an integral approach to Buddhist philosophy, instead of saying that only Madhyamaka has the answer and all the others should be refuted.

Many Madhamakans say that the reason we should not accommodate the other philosophical approaches is because there is something to cling onto. So in their terms: "If we subscribe to the idea of emptiness, there is nothing to cling onto, but if we subscribed to the Yogacara way of thinking, we would have to cling onto the mind, and say that the mind has power over everything else. If we subscribed to the Abhidharma theory, we would be clinging onto the idea of dharmas."

However, if we think of the mind, dharmas, and everything, as not having inherent existence, enduring substance, and so forth, as Madhyamaka describes, and also think, be it on the conventional level, that dharmas do have some reality and that reality is processed and organized by the mind, then we have an integral approach. In other words, dharmas themselves do not have inherent existence because the dharmas are interacting.

Therefore, the dharmas interact and the interaction is organized and made sense of, incorporated into one's mental life, because of the power of the mind. Even though the mind is so powerful and the dharmas are necessary for things to work, nevertheless, they do not have inherent existence. They are devoid of essence and their nature is empty (Skt. *shunya*). In reality they have the nature of emptiness.

If we look at it from an integral point of view, where we have the early Buddhist philosophers saying that dharmas or entities have some reality, and Yogacara philosophy holding the view that everything is dependent on the mind, there is no contradiction. To subscribe to the idea that for things to exist there must be a network of dharmas all mutually impacting on each other, and then also to say that what is perceived in this way is dependent on one's mind—that everything we perceive is dependent on the mind—to see it like this would be the integral approach. Some of the 19th century Tibetan Buddhist masters actually did just that.

This is an example in relation to how we might think about integral Buddhism, using Buddhist philosophy as an example, but we can use this model with the different aspects of Buddhism. We can apply it to Buddhist psychology and we may also want to incorporate Western thought into that model. There is no conflict there either.

When I was involved in dialogue with Ken Wilber, I proposed that the premodern, modern, and post-modern ways of thinking could also be integrated. There is no reason to believe that in order to think like a modern person, we must necessarily free ourselves from premodern ways of thinking: the mythic and mytho-poetic ways of thinking, for example. Further, to think like a modern person but use logic, reason, and rationality—and a respect for science—all the values of Western Enlightenment that the 16th, 17th, and 18th century philosophers and scientists gave us, brings a lot of richness to our mental life. To dispense with that is to be diminished. In addition, we can also think like a post-modernist, so that we do not reify the concepts of reason and rationality, putting them on a pedestal and thinking that reason and rationality is everything. We do not have to do that. As the post-modernists say, our thinking has a lot to do with our cultural surroundings and upbringing and many other things. This also makes sense.

We could incorporate this into our way of living and thinking. We could think in a mytho-poetic way, a rational way, or a more post-modernist way, where we have more respect for diversity and plurality but, at the same time, resist falling into an extreme form of relativism, whether it be cognitive relativism, where there are no knowable truths, or moral relativism, meaning that there is no "one" morality. Morality is dependent on where we are—whatever religion, culture, we were brought up in. That is what dictates what is moral and not moral.

We look at the whole thing from an integral point of view and, in this way, we bring that to the practice of Buddhism, and to Buddhist philosophy and psychology as well.

Section Three
Psychology

14
Psychology, Spirituality, and the Mind

We look at Buddhist psychology from the integral standpoint of being accommodating and encompassing. In Buddhism, mind or psyche has many different levels and dimensions. Therefore, we can also deal with our mind and mental states on many different levels through the approach of Buddhist psychology, which is just one of the many ways to work with our mind.

In the end, in Buddhism, everything boils down to the mind. Buddhist psychology is very important because it is tied up with Buddhist ethics. We cannot have Buddhist ethics without having some understanding of Buddhist psychology. The Buddhist notion of precepts or shila is often mistakenly translated as "ethics." In the precepts it is said that we should not lie, kill, and so on. These are *moral* precepts, and do not constitute the Buddhist notion of ethics. "Ethics," in Buddhism, has a much broader connotation. The precepts are related to certain moral principles that we follow, but ethics are seen as something superior, in a sense, being about the cultivation of goodness in oneself. When we are starting out, we need guidelines and moral principles, but the main point is that we must learn to transform ourselves in relation to our character.

Buddhist ethical training is based on the building of our character through what we call "wholesome activities" because then we will develop the necessary skills to deal with life's issues in a conducive and constructive manner. This is the goal. To transform ourselves in relation to our character, we have to have an understanding of our mind. This is why psychology and Buddhist ethics are so intimately tied to each other.

Understanding Our Mind

Understanding our mind comes about in two ways: observation or paying attention and through insight. Following the practice of mindfulness or paying attention to the mind, in post-meditation situations we need to engage in contemplation and reflection. We try to recollect what it was we were observing so that we can begin to accumulate an understanding of what sorts of things are coming up in the mind.

The reason we need to do this is because everything that we experience is based on causes and conditions, as Buddhism teaches. Our emotional upheavals are connected with the kinds of thoughts that we entertain. This does not mean that thoughts are more important than emotions, but it is about the fact that most of the emotions are there because we think and, in particular, because of the kinds of thoughts we have. We hold certain belief systems about ourselves. It is like a vicious circle. Based on our beliefs about ourselves, different kinds of thoughts arise. If one believes oneself to be unintelligent, then the thoughts one has are going to be about that. Different kinds of life experiences can then act like a triggering mechanism to unleash the kinds of thoughts that confirm one's belief. We end up reconfirming our opinion, saying, "Yes, I am unintelligent, because of this, that, and the other thing." This may then also bring about physical reactions, like tightness in the chest, a rise in body temperature, a faster heartbeat, heart palpitations, dryness of the mouth, or faster breathing. When that occurs, the appropriate emotions would arise, such as frustration, anger, depression, sadness, or whatever the case might be. This will then affect one's behavior. Based on that belief, a person like that may not even try to learn anything or apply themselves to study because they believe that they are incapable of learning. They may think, "That's beyond me. I can't do that. I won't be able to benefit from trying to learn this or that."

It is plain that our thoughts, emotions, feelings, bodily responses, and behavior are interrelated. Due to this, psychology and ethics are intimately tied together. This, then, is how we have to use the Buddhist meditational practices and teachings of Abhidharma. Instead of thinking, "I have anger problems," we need to pay more attention to anger and see *how* we have anger problems. What sort of anger arises? Taking note of that and being very specific about the emotions we experience, the emotional afflictions we have, is the key. We do things like that and then set realistic goals.

Based on such practices as these, one also tries to replace negative thoughts with positive thoughts so that instead of saying, "I wish I could do this or that," for example, one says, "I would like to have such and such a thing happen," or "I would like to do such and such a thing." Basically, we try to rephrase monologues and self-talk we engage in. When we notice the negative feedback we are giving ourselves, we try to rephrase these thoughts in such a way that they have a positive complexion, or at least, are not so negative. The idea is that, as Buddhism says, the thoughts that go through our mind leave imprints. This is part of the process of the karmic imprints. If we rephrase these thoughts, this self-talk, we will feel differently. We will notice this and when we do, we will be encouraged and think, "Yes, I can deal with these things," instead of being overwhelmed.

Whatever negative issue we have to deal with, we can look at it as a whole, but then we try to break it up into parts. This is a very

Buddhist way of working. Right from the beginning, we try to break up whatever it is into parts, and then we look at them individually. We do the same with our emotional states. Then, we may even write them down after mindfulness practice. If we have noticed different things, then we analyze them, break them down and, by doing so, we get more of a sense of what is really going on in our mind. This is an overview of what we need to do, but that is the general idea.

Meditation

We use both shamatha and vipashyana[34] methods. With vipashyana, we are trying to understand what is going on: looking at the interconnections between the thoughts, emotions, feelings, bodily states, and our actions, both verbal and physical. We are paying attention and we have that understanding. That understanding is then cemented or strengthened by paying attention to the sorts of thoughts, feelings, emotions, and bodily reactions we experience and how this manifests, in terms of our behavior.

In that way, one learns to integrate shamatha with vipashyana practice. People often practice vipashyana as if it was shamatha practice—but that is not vipashyana. Vipashyana has to be about thinking, but one must be thinking in the correct fashion. Vipashyana is meant to clarify one's confusion. This does not happen miraculously but has to be developed and cultivated. The way to cultivate it, as I said in chapters 11 and 12, has to come from seeing the interconnected nature of everything. In this case, one also needs to see how different thoughts, emotions, feelings, bodily states, and physical behaviors are interconnected. That is how to do shamatha and vipashyana together. We cannot just practice shamatha without vipashyana because, as it is said in the teachings, even if you practiced shamatha for a thousand years, you would not gain insight. You may become calmer but you would not become wiser. However, if you combine vipashyana with shamatha, then you will become wiser. Gaining wisdom is different from accumulating knowledge because it is about fully comprehending how things are interconnected, how everything impacts on everything else, how, for example even our behavior can impact on our thoughts, emotions, and feelings.

Again, it is like a vicious circle; it goes around in a circle. The purpose of Buddhist practice is to deconstruct that, so that the circle is not repeated and there is some kind of change. The point is that it is very difficult not to have certain emotions but it is slightly easier, although still difficult, to start changing how we think about things. If we start thinking about them differently, almost automatically the emotions and feelings will follow suit. By simply trying to rephrase things, this will have some impact on the emotional, feeling, and physical level. By dealing with these thoughts, then gradually we begin to work with the more fundamental beliefs we have about ourselves. There are different layers. We cannot uproot our basic beliefs about ourselves straight away but, as it is said in the teachings, by dealing with the branches first, gradually we get to the trunk and then to the root. It has to be done in that way because it is the branches that feed the trunk, and the trunk, in turn, keeps the roots flourishing. We have to start from what is immediate.

Instead of thinking too much about one's past experiences, it is much more profitable to think about what is going on now. As Buddhism says, a lot of what is going on in our mind is habitual, which means that whatever was suppressed or repressed a long time ago, cannot be so very different from what we currently experience and think. With this kind of understanding, one tries to deal with what one is experiencing now and then, gradually, as one goes deeper and deeper, one might begin to understand the origin of some of our more fundamental disturbances.

So our approach to psychology in Buddhism involves, as a starting point, identifying our thoughts and emotions but, at the same time, not judging, not thinking, "I have a good thought. I have a bad thought." Do not think like that, because it is not helpful. Just because we have bad thoughts about someone or other does not make us a bad person for having those thoughts, which is the conclusion we may jump to. Our thoughts move so fast: we have one thought, then we jump to another thought, and often those two thoughts do not, in fact, relate. We are actually logically inconsistent. We generalize, we exaggerate, we minimize—we do all kinds of things like that. Our thought pattern is such that we feed ourselves the wrong information and, by doing so, we begin to develop a false sense of self, thinking, "I am this kind of person. I am that kind of person," and so on. It is very important then, to take a pause and isolate each thought and see what kind of thought we are having, what we are thinking, at any moment. We cannot do it all the time; it has never been said that we should do this all the time, but we should do it as often as we can. We do not have to sit on a cushion to do that; it could be when we are sitting on a chair, and it could even be when we are in conversation with somebody. We could be walking, we could be sitting on a bench in the park looking at the ducks swimming in the pond, and taking it all in.

Acceptance

Acceptance of our experiences is the first thing that Buddhism talks about, which means not judging our thoughts. As soon as we judge our experience, we are already judging ourselves because we identify our thoughts, emotions, and feelings with who we are. We jump to conclusions. We say, "I'm a hateful kind of person," "I'm really a very jealous person," or "I'm lustful and greedy." That is one thing. The other is that we may be all of these, yet we do not want to acknowledge it. There is no real acceptance. Avoidance of emotions is a big part of what we have to do in terms of transforming ourselves. It is okay to say, "Yes, I'm jealous. I'm envious. I'm aggressive sometimes. I'm lustful. I am all the bad things, but I am also all the other things." When we are compassionate, when we are loving, when we are caring, we can avoid these less admirable behaviors. When we criticize ourselves too much, then we start to think, "I'm not loving enough. I don't care enough. I am not the person that I want to be." Again, we beat ourselves up.

So, from the start, what we need to learn, in terms of Buddhist psychology, is acceptance of myriad experiences—good, bad, or ugly. Anything that we experience is okay. No harm is done. There is absolutely no harm in experiencing things and acknowledging them. As I said in a previous chapter, Buddhism explains that the reason we suffer is because we do not have enough insight into our lives. When we acknowledge what is really going on, there is knowledge, because we can see ourselves doing many things: some we may approve of, and others we may not approve of. However, some kind of fundamental acceptance is needed. This does not give us license to do whatever we feel like doing. It just gives us the freedom to finally look at ourselves, warts and all, and say, "Well, this is me, it is okay." We give some kind of reassurance to ourselves when we say, "Yes, I have my flaws. Who doesn't?" We all have flaws. We just say, "I have flaws. I have some shortcomings and that's me and it is okay." This is the fundamental starting point, otherwise there can be no real change. We cannot really change if we do not have that sense of self-acceptance because without that there is no starting point. Once we accept ourselves in that way, we can say, "Sometimes I get jealous. Sometimes I am envious. Sometimes I am lustful. Sometimes I am greedy. Sometimes I am needy. Sometimes I am compassionate. I care. I have many positive feelings. I also feel a lot of joy and happiness." So we look at everything, all the things that we do and do not like ourselves doing.

Attraction and Aversion

This is an important topic because, as Buddhism says, what it comes down to at the end, in terms of human psychology, is that there are three kinds of driving forces. Ignorance is the primary factor, which I mentioned previously, and the other two are attraction and aversion. Everything that we do is based on attraction and aversion. We are attracted to doing certain things, and have aversion to doing others. With what we hear, what we see, what we smell, what we taste, and what we touch, we push some things away and with others, we think, "I want this." We are like that poor little creature, Gollum in the Lord of the Rings. I am not actually exaggerating all that much. When we want something, we want it so much. With aversion, we will not even take a second look, but if we were to look again, it could be good. For example, sometimes one can go to a secondhand store and pick up a treasure, something really nice such as a fantastic painting. Initially, we may have thought everything was cheap trash so we walked by and we lost our opportunity right there. However, if we had taken notice, we would have seen what was there among all the other stuff. It happens like that, even with other human beings, with human interaction, and our life experiences generally. Isolating things and paying attention to what we experience is the fundamental way to start.

Misunderstanding

After we begin to make some headway in terms of isolating things and moderating our responses, we have to think that what we experience is not factually based. It is based on what we *think* is going on. We believe that what we decide is going on is what is actually happening, but it is not really what is going on. We have a "take on it," in other words. How many times do we go out with a group of people and we could be talking about art, justice, human rights, or natural law—we bring these things up and we do not all agree, because we are coming from different points of view? There is nothing wrong with that, but it is good to know that is what is happening.

Then we have to extend that idea into our own emotional and psychological life and think, "Yes, I think that they are like this and that, but that's only my feeling based on my own experience. It may be true or it may not be true." Sometimes we get hung up on the idea of truth but truth is not the most important thing. What is most important is what brings the best result, what benefits the most people, and so we can begin by asking if it is bringing benefit to us or to the other person. It is important to do that, instead of always trying to push the idea that "I have to be right and I have to prove the other person wrong." We just keep on doing that in our somnambulant state.

With that in mind, we can see it is very important to actually accept what we feel. Acceptance is fundamental. The next stage in the process is recognizing the degree to which we interpret our experiences. Our experiences are not given as hard facts. We interpret them. We think that somebody is looking at us in this or that way. We make all kinds of interpretations of other people's gestures. We may think that communication has only to do with words, but words play a very small role in how we relate to somebody. The eyes, the gestures, and what the person projects—all of those are so important. That is how our emotions become aroused. It is not simply because something or other is said. If somebody says something quite nasty to us with not much of a physical component to it—for example, if we are in a line and they say to us, "Could you just move?" we will say, "Okay." However, if someone were to say it very aggressively, then it is not just what has been said, but how it has been said, the words that have been used, or the physical posture that has been adopted, that feed into our interpretation. Then we have to go along with that, in a sense. In any case, it is dependent on interpretation. We may think a person using expletives is being aggressive but, still, we do not know whether they are really angry or just acting up. It could be the case that the one in our example who is not saying much has problems expressing anger, and the other person who is carrying on is just letting off steam and may not be so angry. However, we may interpret it in the opposite way.

We have to put it in context. What kind of person is this? How would they behave with their friends, and with their spouse, and so on? If someone is spewing anger then you have a problem, but what I am trying to say is that interpretation is always operating. How we relate to people has so much to do with how we read people and their gestures. Often we get it wrong. It is very important to observe how people behave. If they do not mean anything harmful by their behavior, then we do not have to take a lot of notice, but if somebody actually means to do us harm, then we will be able to notice that too. We will be more alert and able to see who may be trying to do us harm and who is actually harmless. A parallel situation could be where we need to interpret if the dog that barks a lot actually does not bite and, conversely, whether the one that does not bark, in fact, bites.

If we interpret to a degree that is not necessary, however, it becomes not only useless, but also disabling. The way of thinking that exaggerates, minimizes, or generalizes is a hindrance to leading a normal life, a meaningful life, a life imbued with purpose and meaning. Anxiety, depression, and paranoia follow from thinking like that, because we lose faith or belief. It is really important to believe in something, whether it is Buddhism, or something else. With that as the central point, everything we do should emanate from there.

Bringing everything back to that center is so very important because if we do not believe in anything, we will have nothing but despair. These days, many people seem to have almost given up on things, and whatever excitement they do experience holds only the status of a sound byte. As long as we have somebody we are connected with on Facebook or Twitter, we say it is "all good" but, fundamentally, we may not be feeling all that good in ourselves. There is no face-to-face connection with others and obviously, as human beings, we cannot live without other people, without real, living human beings. To rely only on the hundreds of people we may talk to on the Internet, we really cannot achieve that. Face-to-face connection is crucial and, through that, we interpret what is happening. We have to deal with that.

As we have already discussed, acceptance holds great importance within Buddhist psychology and it applies not only to acceptance of what we feel, but to acceptance of what we do in relation to other people and, in turn, to how we are treated by other people—what other people do to us, in a manner of speaking. Our discussion, then, has been exploring the significance of interpretation and we have identified the pitfalls of faulty interpretation, where exaggeration, minimization, and generalization lead to anxiety, depression, and paranoia. The next step of the process is to look at ourselves, the agent who experiences these things. Who do you think is depressed? Who do you think is angry? Who do you think is anxious? Who do you think is disappointed? Who do you think is frustrated in terms of looking ahead to frustrated goals? So, turning our attention to ourselves, looking into ourselves, we say, "Who is the person having these experiences?" When we do that, we do not have to think there is this "me," this tiny little baby almost. There is no regression being talked about here. We just look at what is really going on right now. Right now in my present life,

I look at myself and when I do not like something, when there is somebody I do not like, who I think has done some harm to me, I think to myself, "What is this me that is being harmed?"

Letting Go and Sense of Self

If we really analyze it properly, there is not one single thing called "me." There is just the feeling of harm that we have experienced, which is what we have to address. "I" am not being harmed. The feeling of harm that I have experienced is what I have to address. This is the mistake that we always fall into. We think, "I have been harmed, and so-and-so has done this to me and that to me." Incidentally, I have used some of the techniques that I know and it really does help, because I am not thinking, "I am this person and I am being harmed." I contextualize, I see it in context, and sometimes I even give credence to the person trying to do me harm, by thinking, "Well, maybe there was some reason to do it, even though, from my point of view, the reasons were a bit warped." This is most important—that it is all only from my point of view. Then I let go.

Letting go is the main point. We have to see ourselves in a dynamic situation and, if people make a criticism, we have to look at whether the criticism has some basis or not. If so, we should take that on board, and it will help us to change. And if the criticism has no basis, we do not have to call that person an idiot. We do not have to use expletives. It is not necessary. We just let it rest and say, "Well, if that is how you feel, that is fine. That's no problem." However, we should not do it in a dismissive manner. This is so important. We need to see ourselves as always changing and if people help us to change, whether they are being supportive or not—even if they are not supportive, if we have the ears to listen, they may actually have said something that we need to hear, even though it may not be pleasant.

It is similar to what I was saying before, in relation to thoughts, feelings, and emotions. When thoughts, feelings, and emotions flood our mind during meditation, we do not like it, but we have to accept that. Similarly, when people—especially someone who actually cares about us—say certain things with the intention of being helpful, it is good to take heed, to pay attention. Then we change. With some people, we can say that we think we know everything and have sorted it all out, but others may actually be saying things that we need to take on board. I really believe this and it is what Buddhism says. Then, through using that approach, we are able to see the self as a changing thing, in context, because we know we do not have a fixed self. There is no such thing as "me." I am what I am at any given time. When we were one year old or three years old, we were completely different from what we are now.

It is not about, "What is the real me? What was 'me' when I was born?" We were born with nothing. We were a helpless and hapless creature. We grew into adulthood, then we aged, and we will finally die, but planning for all of this is the key in Buddhism. In psychology—and I think it is a Hindu idea—they talk about the four stations of life, and I think this is a good approach. We are encouraged to work and earn money and have a good life; we should pursue the Dharma, as that is a really good basis, and we should enjoy pleasure (Skt: *kama*). So we have pleasure, we do all of that, and it makes our life whole, according to Hinduism—and Buddhism is very close to Hinduism. Living a good life, living a life that is ethical, living a life that is spiritual—that is what it is all about. Hinduism does not say this but, for us, as Buddhists in that context, we have to see ourselves as changing, and as able to adapt. Adaptability is important because, as a biologist too would say, it is the species that adapts that will survive, and those that cannot adapt, perish. As human beings, if we can adapt, think in a new way, and continue like that, we will flourish as a result; if we do not adapt, then we may believe we are young in our thinking but, in effect, we will be old, because we are stuck and not moving. According to Buddhist psychology, we should not end up like that.

Spirituality and Psychology

Another point to address in relation to psychology in Buddhism, is that we need to make a distinction between psychology and spirituality. Psychology is about the mind. In terms of spirituality, although in Buddhism we do not have the idea of "spirit" or "soul" or anything like that, nevertheless, there is the idea of what in Zen Buddhism they call "big mind" or "no mind" and, in Mahamudra and Dzogchen, "mind-in-itself." This is important to think about. Here, in this context, it is not about trying to be anything. There is no conflict between, on the one hand, trying to be what you wish to be, and, on the other, being yourself and not trying to *be* anything. You try to be whatever you wish to be but, ultimately, it does not really matter in the end. You may be whatever you are. It is okay, everything is okay, everything is fine—that is the spiritual perspective, and it comes with the idea of "big mind" or "mind-in-itself," because it is spacious and accommodating. Nothing matters, basically.

If you have watched the Chögyam Trungpa Rinpoche documentary, "Crazy Wisdom," "crazy wisdom" is like that. In the end, it does not matter. Everything is good. It is not nihilistic. It is nothing like the situation where "nothing matters" means that we think, "I may just as well be dead." Instead, nothing matters in this context because everything is good, which is the opposite. You celebrate everything that is going on. You see even the bad things that go on as the display of the phenomena. This is what it is called, actually, in the language of Mahamudra and Dzogchen. We use those words: "display of the phenomena." If there are people fighting and shouting at each other and carrying on, you would just look at it and say, "Oh, that is just another display of the phenomena." This is no joke, actually. It is a display of the phenomena and sort of crazy in one respect, but not really crazy. Many people have said a lot of things about Trungpa Rinpoche, about his craziness, but I do not think he was that crazy at all.

Contextualizing of the Self

It is all about context. The contextualization of one's self is a really important component in our lives, because then we can see ourselves in this context or that—when I am in this situation, I act this way, and when I am in that situation, I act that way. We do not necessarily ask, "Which one is the real me?" We have to act. What we have to do, basically, is present some kind of persona. In our work environment, we act in one way, and with our friends, we may act in a different way. With our spouse, we act in yet another way. This is a good thing, and we are not thinking about which one is the real "me." We own up to all of that and say, "See, really, I can do all of that. I am good at work, and I get on with people. I talk with the customers nicely. I have friends, and I get on well with them. I do my best to get on with my spouse. But I have to play different roles. I can't behave the way I do at work, when I am home. I can't pretend that I am with my friend when I am with my spouse, and I can't treat my colleague like my spouse, because then I might get into trouble."

Consequently, we can see why contextualizing is very important. It is rarely acknowledged but we somehow instinctively accept and accommodate the different roles required of us in leading our lives. The roles we inhabit in a work context, a family context, in our various friendships, and so on seem to be accommodated but, in the context of spirituality, where it is critical that we are able to look into and acknowledge all aspects of ourselves, we struggle. Spiritual insight is different from psychological insight. The spiritual insight we gain from practicing Mahamudra, Dzogchen, and teachings like these is far superior to any psychological method because, as the teachings say, there are no methods. However, for us to get to that level of spiritual insight we do have to employ methods. We need to use the methods I have been discussing, to get to that level of accomplishment but, once we have reached that level, then there are no methods. The thought of employing methods to attain Mahamudrahood is a joke, really. We cannot do it. There are no methods. How would you get into the uncontrived, natural state of being by using methods? We cannot do that. Because we have so many hurdles to overcome, so many obstacles, we have to do these things but, ultimately, none of them would be necessary if we could be in our natural state. We would then be at peace with ourselves. That is all.

We would not have to identify what I am thinking, what I am feeling, what I am desiring, what I am remembering, what I am anticipating, where I am at, who I am dating, what the person I am dating is like. It would not concern us in the least because we have become wandering yogis. We would have an "I don't give a damn" attitude—but not of the "Frankly, my dear, I don't give a damn" kind, like Clark Gable in the movie, *Gone with the Wind*.

To think about spirituality in the right way is imperative, because spirituality is not about any "thing." Thinking about anything as a "thing" is the problem. As soon as we start to think about it as a "thing," we turn it into something material and it is not spiritual. Spirituality has nothing to do with any "thing," whether ideal or real. It is not like a tangible object that we can hang onto, like a car or a big house. The importance of spirituality cannot be overstated and, again, it is not about any "thing." In relation to spirituality, we cannot hang onto anything. Nothing is as important as just being; simply being is the most important thing. It is without striving, without struggle, without scrambling after something or other. It is simply just being: being content and being happy. This does not mean we cannot think about the state of the world, or take social action. It is about how we are in ourselves, not about what we do.

If we are like that in ourselves, then whatever we do will emanate from that.

It is this element that I referred to earlier, in relation to the Chögyam Trungpa Rinpoche documentary, "Crazy Wisdom." If you are like that in yourself, then whatever you do will emanate from that and it will always be good. That is the fundamental thing and that is also the crazy wisdom idea. You are not judging, you are not thinking, "It has to be like this." It is nothing like that. You are very sharp. You are clear. And if you do not support something—for example, if you do not support war and terror, then you can say, "I don't support that," but you do not have to agonize over what you cannot do. You focus on what you can do. There is so much you can do to help with that situation, if you are against war and terror. You can do many things, so why waste time thinking about what you cannot do? You need to go and find out what you can do. I am using an extreme example but I know there are many people with strong feelings about these things so somebody might ask me, "What do you do in a circumstance like that when you have a Mahamudra or Dzogchen point of view?" This is my answer: it does not mean you do not do anything and sit idly by and think, "This world has gone to the dogs."

Spirituality is the answer. Psychology can only help on a temporary basis. If we really need liberation, then it is spirituality that will give us that. Spirituality is the answer, not psychology. Psychology is like putting a dressing on a wound. If you fall over and get a wound on your knee, then you put a patch on. It does not matter whether it is a psychoanalytic, humanistic, existential, or cognitive psychotherapist. Even now, when there is a Buddhist influence, with mindfulness-focused therapy and so on, it is always about modifying your mind. Mindfulness-focused therapy is about trying to change your mind. Buddhism talks about this also, but what I am trying to say is that, in the end, spirituality is about not doing anything. It is about just being yourself and being in yourself and accepting all your aspects, being happy about being what you are. This is the spiritual perspective in Buddhism. Mahamudra and Dzogchen say, "Be in your natural state. Do not be in a contrived state of being. Be free of acceptance and rejection." We want to accept certain positive experiences, even in meditation, but we need to look at this more closely.

We say, "I like this. I was meditating and I had this fantastic experience. I saw my father—who is no longer here with me—but I saw him and he was glowing and it was so beautiful." Well, that is great, but let us get back to the nitty-gritty of things. Spirituality is about accepting all aspects of ourselves—without acceptance and rejection. No acceptance, no rejection, no acceptance, no rejection—and we actually have to drum that into our heads—no acceptance, no rejection... It works. Why? It is because, then, we do not have to accept bad things. That is no acceptance. As well as that, we do not have to reject bad things in a forceful and unhappy fashion. You do not accept, but you do not reject. This is a very subtle idea and very difficult to do, in fact. But we should all attempt to do that: not accepting all the bad things, but also not rejecting them. We should do the same thing with our feelings, emotions, and psychological states. Not rejecting, but not accepting—just leaving it. We do not say, "Oh, that's me. I'm greedy, so bad." We accept our greediness but then we also do not say, "Oh, I'm greedy and that's that." This is what it means: you accept, but you do not reject. "Non-acceptance, non-rejection" means that.

Integral Psychology

We can see, therefore, that not everything about the mind is psychological. Everything to do with psychological states is mental, of course, but not everything that is mental is psychological. There are states of being which go beyond the psychological states, which go beyond, transcend, our normal psychological states of being. So, in other words, they go beyond mental states of all kinds, beyond our thoughts, emotions, feelings, and varieties of cognitive processes.

This is a very important point because at the core of our mental life is what we call our nature of the mind. We call this the "big mind" or "buddha-nature" or the "mind of clear light." Whatever we call it, that description of our mental life goes beyond the psychological. This is most important to think about. If we adopt the integral approach in relation to psychology, this has to be taken into account: we are incorporating all the different levels of the mind.

SECTION FOUR

Health and Well-being

15

Prana and Pranayama

Before we begin discussion of prana and pranayama,[35] we will first look at where the practice of pranayama is found in the larger scheme of things. It is drawn from Tantrayana or Vajrayana in Tibetan Buddhism, which is not a separate school as such, but an extension of Mahayana. Accordingly, Vajrayana is not separate from Mahayana, since Mahayana is divided into two segments, which are the exoteric and esoteric aspects, the esoteric aspect being Vajrayana. Sometimes we talk about the three yanas or three vehicles of Buddhism, being the Shravakayana, Mahayana, and Tantrayana and, at a glance, that may give us the impression that Vajrayana or Tantrayana is separate from Mahayana. However, as we can see, that is not so and Vajrayana is actually within Mahayana, in terms of representing the esoteric aspect of Mahayana, but otherwise it is the same philosophy. It is the same everything, except that in Vajrayana we do not think about delaying enlightenment. If we can achieve enlightenment more quickly, then we should do so. Simply because we follow the Mahayana path, we do not need to think, "I should not strive to attain enlightenment for myself. I should be putting others first. That should really be my priority."

Tantrayana says that this is not the way to think about it.

There are differences in terms of method, between the exoteric and esoteric forms of Mahayana but, in terms of view—that is, in terms of philosophy, in terms of what we have been discussing—there is no difference. We still make use of the teachings of Nagarjuna, Chandrakirti, Asanga, and Vasubhandu but, again, the difference lies in the techniques that are employed. Therefore, in Tantrism, we use techniques that are not to be found in traditional exoteric Mahayana. We make use of visualization practices, we do yoga practices, pranayama practices, and so on. It is said that Vajrayana is rich in method, rich in skillful means.

The pranayama practices, then, are associated with Vajrayana, but we need to distinguish between the types of Vajrayana practices. Tibetan Buddhism itself is divided into the old school and the new school, the old school being Nyingma, while the new school includes the remaining three schools of Tibetan Buddhism: Kagyu, Sakya, and Gelug. According to the new school, Tantrayana can be divided into four divisions, which are: *Kriya tantra*, *Charya tantra*, *Yoga tantra*, and *Anuttarayoga tantra*. Pranayama is taken from the last division, the *Anuttarayoga tantra*. *Anuttarayoga* means the "supreme yoga," since it is the most esoteric, most advanced yoga.

The four tantras are classified into what is emphasized most, in relation to body, speech, and mind. The lower tantras focus more on the body and speech aspects and less on the mental aspect and this is why there is particular emphasis on the precision with which the rituals and recitation of mantras are performed and on the purity of one's diet and of the rituals. Those are called "outer tantras" and the two higher tantras, especially the last one, are called "inner tantras" because they focus more on the inner aspect. Pranayama is seen as one of the inner practices. Even though physicality is involved, still, it is an inner practice, according to Tantrayana. To perform the entire practice, as in *Anuttarayoga tantra*, you would need tantric initiation to begin with and then you would be required to do various tantric *sadhana*[36] practices. It is quite legitimate, however, to do only the pranayama or some of the yogic exercises. I would like to make that clear because otherwise it might be thought that these practices were being taught "willy-nilly." More and more lamas say that it has a legitimate use in such a context and, as a result, many lamas are now teaching these practices. So this is just a brief overview of how pranayama fits into the tantric framework.

Looking at every aspect of the body goes hand in hand with how Buddhism says we need to think about and approach the totality of our body and mind. So, in terms of the body, we can say that without all the different parts and systems that comprise it, we have no body. When it comes to pranayama and health, what we have to think about is the inner structure of our body in relation to prana, *nadis*, and *chakras*. We may be short or tall, we may be thin or weighty, but those issues are of no consequence in the Tibetan Buddhist health system. Instead, we think about getting in touch with our energy centers, energy pathways, and the vital energy that flows through them. By thinking like that, we become more in tune with what we are as a human being. We may get caught up with the external world, with how we look, how we appear to other people, but we generally do not pay attention to what really goes on inside our body. Chakras are energy centers. We have chakras in the head, the throat, the heart, the navel, and just above the sex organ. So we have these various energy centers in the body and I am sure that, at times, we are aware of them. Sometimes we feel tension in the head or we feel dizzy and we have different experiences relating to that and to the vocal aspect, in terms of how well our voice is working. Not just in Buddhism but also in the Indian way of thinking generally, the vocal aspect, exercising our vocal capacity, is of great importance. The heart chakra is where the emotions lie, according to the Hindu and Buddhist way of thinking—not just love and what we often associate the heart with, but also jealousy, anger, resentment, and so on and, at that time, a lot of tension, a lot of anxiety is held at that chakra. When we feel anxious, when we suffer anxiety, where do we feel that? We feel it there. Many of the things that are spoken about are not abstract; they correspond to how we actually feel, how we literally experience things.

When we get confused, we may even physically feel it in the head; we may even hit our head and say, "I'm such an idiot." Sometimes, if we have had a fantastic experience or a fantastic time with someone then we might say, "My head is going to explode!" We say that because we feel that. Experiences like these seem to have parallels with regard to the location of the crown chakra. When we feel as if somebody has betrayed us, we might say, "I feel as though I have been stabbed in the heart"—even though the person has not done that. So that is in reference to the heart chakra.

It is very beneficial to practice pranayama because it will calm our nerves. It does not mean, however, that we will stop experiencing things, that it will somehow numb our reactions. In fact, we will experience things in ways that are helpful rather than harmful. There will be more joy, more pleasure. This kind of teaching does not say that pleasure is a bad thing; instead, it says it is the fixation on pleasure, fixation generally, which stops us enjoying ourselves. Learning to activate the chakras, activating our crown chakra, throat chakra, heart chakra, and navel chakra, for example, will allow us to enjoy all our sensory experiences in a way that is not harmful. When that is not happening, often what we experience becomes harmful, but if the chakras are activated, then it is not harmful, because we are able to experience things for what they are, instead of conceptualizing, thinking, "Is this real? What does that mean? What is going on?" We should not think that but just be in that state, just experience whatever it is we are experiencing. This is fundamental and it is very important to take note of because when we have good experiences, often we cannot just leave it alone. So that is the chakra aspect.

Prana

When we come to look at prana, we have what we call "upward-moving" prana and "downward-moving" prana. The upward-moving prana is what is operating when we hiccup, regurgitate, or vomit. So with regard to having eaten something that is not good for us, the body will automatically react, so we will vomit. Downward-moving prana is operating when we have to go to the toilet to defecate, relieve ourselves. It is prana that allows us to do that. These are the two principal pranas that are spoken of. So when we do pranayama, we are working with these two within the pranic system. I want to speak about this in a polite manner. If we cannot vomit, let us say, then our pranic system is not working very well, and if we suffer constipation then, likewise, our pranic system is not functioning properly—toxicity is present so then our body is not cleansed. In India, they take enemas to correct such a problem, and that is what might be needed if one has not been doing pranayama. If our prana system were working, one would not need enemas.

If we are able to modify our body temperature, that means that our prana is working. Sometimes when we have a meal, our body becomes heated up and at other times our body gets cold, but if we are able to use our pranic practice, then despite what we eat, we can actually monitor our body temperature. We can cool down when it is hot outside, and we can heat up our body in cold conditions. This is no myth. When it is really cold, you are able to heat your body up, and when it is hot it is possible to lower your body temperature. You really can do this. If you practice it you will be surprised. It is not actually so difficult to do. Another approach we can take is eating certain foods to heat us up or to cool us down.

Basically, eating meat will heat us up and eating vegetables will cool us down. There are also dietary remedies for anemia, for example, but I will not list here the names of the foods one might have to eat.

When we are feeling agitated, anxious, worried, we may decide to get into vigorous exercise, such as jogging, as a way of dealing with the problem, but that is not good for us. Temporarily, one might feel some relief, but it will last for only a few minutes and then one will find the agitation is still there. What you really need is massage, relaxation. You should go to a massage therapist; you have to cool down. You do not need to go to a gym and carry on, to jump on a treadmill or anything like that. Instead, you slow down. You have a massage. *Kumnye*—that is what you need. You cool yourself down, you feel good, relaxed, and that is what is needed. People who are agitated might decide, "I need to exercise" and having done so may, for a few seconds, think, "Ah, this is good," but then, after a short while, they are just as anxious and restless. Again, this is not good, because you need to calm yourself. You do not jog. You do not get on the treadmill. You just relax. This is very important to remember.

If you do not do anything very physical, if you are a "couch potato," as they say, then you should exercise. You should jump on the treadmill, and you should run—or even just walk, even if it is walking in the street. You should do these things because you will feel invigorated. You will feel energized through walking, and you will also walk with confidence. Walking, exercising, you must do these things and when you exercise, you exercise all aspects of your body. You need to pay attention to all aspects of your arms—biceps, triceps, trapezius muscles, all of those. Sometimes when we exercise, we only focus on the "good parts." We want to show our good aspects, whatever that might be. You may want to show off your "pecs" or, if you have big biceps, you will want to wear your T-shirt and show them off. Of course, if you have good calf muscles, you will want to display them too.

The Buddhist approach to health addresses all aspects of body and mind. The components of each aspect work in parallel, in relationship, with the others. Without all the vital organs, our nervous system, our brain and so on, there is no body. It is the same with the mind. We have to think about things in that way when we are looking at prana, nadis, and the chakra system.

When we touch something, the reason we are able to feel if it is hot or cold is because of prana in the body. All-permeating prana is spread throughout the body to its extremities. It is all-pervasive, all-permeating prana. Again, we need to take this seriously because when this kind of prana is not working well, we will develop arthritic problems and have numbness in our hands, our joints, and we may lose mobility. In short, we will have a problem using our hands and legs properly. We develop these problems because the all-pervasive prana has become restricted.

Buddhism says that the flow of prana can often become entangled and knotted at different points; the heart, head, throat, and navel chakras can become knotted. Basically, we could say that the nadi system is something like the arteries or the nervous system, yet quite different in significant ways. At the different levels, the nadis, which are the conveyers of prana, become entangled and develop knots. Sometimes, for instance, we may develop a heart condition because we have a problem with the nadis. In relation to the throat, sometimes we may lose our voice because our throat chakra is disabled, due to knots forming in the throat. Many people have been known to lose their capacity to speak, despite never having had throat cancer or anything like that. They simply lose their voice and can hardly be heard. If the problem is to do with the head chakra being affected by tangles and knots, then we cannot think. We become irrational, crazy. We say all kinds of things and think they are all real. When we have a lot of anxiety, a lot of issues, we just "feel it in our gut," as people say, so a similar kind of thing happens in the stomach area and there is a reason for that. The channel knots are entangled and we have not learned how to untangle them and so, as a result, we may even develop stomach cancer or the like.

The benefit to us of practicing pranayama is that it will cleanse our body, and it will either cool us down or heat us up, depending on how we do our pranayama. We can do gentle pranayama to cool us down or, if we do vigorous pranayama, it will invigorate us and heat us up. We have to do it like that. So even though you are doing the same pranayama, you do it in relation to what you need, whether it is calmness or invigoration. Again, when you are seeking calmness because you are feeling agitated, you do gentle pranayama and, when you are lacking energy and need invigoration, you do vigorous pranayama, and then you are ready to go! It is also helpful to rub your palms together vigorously. It is really simple, but it is good. It will invigorate you. At home when you are exercising, you can do that when you want to invigorate yourself.

It is imperative for us to practice pranayama for health. It is more beneficial than the exercises we do. The exercises should be used as support for our pranayama practice and not the other way around; we should never think of pranayama as supporting our exercises. Perhaps we may think that we should do more exercise, and then follow it up with a little bit of pranayama, but it should not be like that. We should actually spend most of the time doing pranayama, and then do our exercises, and we will see the result. When we do pranayama, we will feel more in relation to our natural states, and we will be able to see how to heat up and cool down, because we will feel it—but when we exercise we do not experience much, in relation to our bodily feelings.

When we do vigorous physical exercise, we are not really in touch with our feelings. We may be off somewhere in our head and just doing our physical thing. But if we do pranayama, it will really bring the body and mind together. This is why we do pranayama. Breath, prana, is the link that brings the body and mind together. As tantric teachings in Buddhism say, "The breath is the vehicle that the mind rides on." The mind, breath, and body are intimately related. When we are agitated, we breathe in one way, and when we are calm, we breathe in another. If we pay attention to how we breathe at any given time, day or night, we will see the difference. How we breathe reflects what is in our mind. When we are anxious, agitated, worried, or angry, we breathe in a particular way. Our breathing pattern changes all the time. That is prana. Doing pranayama, then, allows us to breathe in a way that is more consistent so that when we are agitated, our breathing does not vary very much.

We could say that, basically, at the stage I have described, we have learned to regulate our breathing. We have control over how we breathe. Normally, we do not know how to breathe; we just leave it to the body. We just breathe and take no notice. But through pranayama, we can learn to regulate our breathing so we have control. This will not stop us falling in love. I am not saying that at all. We will still have these experiences if we do pranayama. So I am not saying that if we do pranayama we will no longer experience anything like that. We will still experience all the emotions, but it will be more regulated. We will have more control. Pranayama will allow us to modify our emotional responses, but we will still feel the intensity—we will still feel that, but without the disturbances that come with it. The enjoyment, all the good things that come with these strong emotions will not diminish. It is only the disturbances accompanying the enjoyable things that will no longer be there.

It is essential to think about it like this, because people might think that it means: "I can't enjoy things. I have to curb these desires, these emotions." It is not like that. We can have these emotions just like we always did, except we will experience things in a different way because we have learnt to use pranayama. We are not so needy or greedy, for example. This is because, normally, when we have a great, intense, emotional experience, we immediately get desirous. We become needy: "I want this. I want it again and again." Then the experience we had becomes diminished, as a result. But if we are not like that anymore, we can have the same experience again and again and it will still be as fresh and good as it was the first time. When we get muddled in our head, and try to repeat the same "fantastic" experience that we had the first time, we have gone down the wrong path. There is no pranayama and we are breathing differently. If we look at ourselves, we will see that. Our thinking is wrong—"Oh, it is not the same, but I want the same experience"—so we try and try and try, in so many ways: "Why? How can I have that experience again?"

However, if we do pranayama, we can have that experience again and again. You are not conceptualizing. There is no *prapanca*—prapanca meaning "conceptual elaboration." There is no prapanca so you are with it. You are with your experience. You are with whatever is there in front of you. You are with whomever you are with. Then everything opens up and you are ready for almost anything, because you have an open, welcoming attitude. Pranayama really does that. Pranayama opens our body up so then our mind becomes more open. When our prana is locked in, it is totally locked in, and we become paranoid. We think everybody is out to get us, or if we see two people are talking, we think they are talking about us.

Prana, Nadi, and Chakras

The nadi aspect is connected to various forms of tantric visualization practices. We will not go into this aspect in great detail so, for now, visualizing or thinking of just the three central channels, and including the four or five chakras, is the main thing. Again, these details are not fixed because it depends on which tantric practice we are doing. There are slight variations in the number of chakras, and the way the nadis or psychophysical energy pathways are structured, in terms of how they link together and so on. This is why I do not think we need to get caught up with the details. In any case, in all the literature, they talk about the three principal nadis.

The central channel (Skt. *avadhuti*), the main channel, basically starts from roughly three inches below the navel, and goes straight up into one's crown. The opening at the crown is often described as flaring out, opening out, like a loudspeaker, and it is said to have a reddish hue inside and to be whitish on the outside.

On either side of and parallel to the central channel are the nadis. Again, the concept, "nadi," does not mean something physical in the real sense, but it describes how the subtle body is constructed. Tantrism says that, apart from the gross body there is also a subtle body, so the subtle body is described in this way, as having nadis or energy pathways or, as sometimes translated, "channels." If you prefer that translation, you can call them "channels," but I call them "energy pathways" because that is how the energy of the prana is directed. The concept of nadi is rather like the Jungian idea of anima and animus. Sometimes it has been compared to the Jungian idea, not only in terms of the psychophysical energy aspect, but also the aspect of life essence and so on. The left nadi (Skt. *lalana*) is described as white in color and it represents the male aspect of one's being. On the right, the other nadi, which is called *rashana* and is red in color, represents the feminine aspect of one's being.

Of course, at the crown, throat, heart, and navel are the psychophysical energy centers, the chakras. At each of the chakras, there are nadis crisscrossing one another. In our unenlightened state, it is said that the prana becomes trapped at these different locations and, as a result, we become disturbed. This is because prana and mind are intimately related. This is the tantric view. Mind and sentience, I suppose. We should not be thinking of mind in too developed a sense, but as sentience. The prana and the sense of being alive are intimately related. When the prana is disturbed, then the mind is disturbed. Even if the mind is not extremely disturbed, nevertheless, simply because there are blockages it means we have all kinds of problems, both physical and mental. Therefore, doing pranayama practice is seen as very helpful.

As I alluded to earlier, sometimes, in certain practices, there is another chakra spoken of, which is called the "secret chakra," corresponding to the genital area. Now, in relation to the prana that travels through these nadis and chakras, five primary and five secondary pranas or *vayu* are mentioned, vayu literally meaning "wind." The wind element has many different layers or levels. We have the gross level of wind, which we can feel externally and internally, but other types of wind are very subtle and cannot be felt, since they are not tangible when in the form of prana.

Five Primary Pranas

There are five primary pranas mentioned, the first of which is called prana vayu (Tib. *soklung*), which means the "prana that sustains life." It is the most powerful of the five and it basically keeps us alive. The second prana is *apana vayu* (Tib. *thursel*), which means "downward or descending prana." The third one, *udana vayu*, is called *gyengyu* in Tibetan, which means "ascending prana," while the fourth is known as *samana vayu* (Tib. *nyamnge*[37]), samana meaning "prana of evenness" or "balance." The fifth and final prana is *vyana vayu* (Tib. *khyapje*), which means "all-pervasive prana." All but the all-pervasive prana have specific locations where they predominantly reside.

The prana vayu, or life-sustaining prana, is located in the heart chakra. It controls our breathing—our inhalation and exhalation—

and keeps the mind and body connected. It is said that this prana supports certain mental tendencies, such as the perception of our own selfhood. It also allows us to remember things, to retain things in our consciousness, in terms of experiences. If this prana became blocked, if there were interference of some kind and it was unable to function properly, then many undesirable physical symptoms or effects would arise, such as fainting, nervousness, and so on.

The ascending or upward-moving prana (Tib. *gyengyu*) helps us to swallow things, to exercise our vocal chords, and it also assists with our breathing. Basically, all the functions that our throat performs are instigated by this prana. Its primary location is the throat center or chakra, and if this prana became impeded or blocked, one could develop upper body problems, such as neck, shoulder, and chest ailments.

The function of downward prana is to enable the discharge of various physical wastes in solid and liquid forms, such as bowel movements and urination. The body is purified of various waste materials by separating and processing them. When this prana becomes blocked, then problems to do with the lower portion of one's body can develop, such as genital diseases, bowel and intestinal problems, gastric disorders, and so on. This prana resides in the genital area, just below the abdominal area.

The prana of evenness has the function of helping to digest food. The digestive system works in such a way that it separates or extracts the nutrients from what has been ingested. What is not nutritious is separated and expelled. If the prana is blocked, we can suffer from gastrointestinal disorders, where our stomach can become bloated and make all kinds of noises. Stomach ulcers can develop from malfunction of this type of prana.

The function of all-pervasive prana is to enable motor activity: our limb movements, joint movements, and so forth. Walking and sitting down are possible because of this prana. As it is all-pervasive, it is present throughout the body, especially at the various large joints, such as the elbows and knees, making movement easier. Blockage of this prana, then, will obviously result in lack of or difficulty of movement. This completes the description of the five primary pranas.

Five Secondary Pranas

The five primary pranas are supported by what are known as the "five secondary pranas," which are described predominantly in terms of their movements. They are associated with the sense organs of the body, enabling them to work well. They are also associated with different elements. In this particular instance, we are not talking about elements in terms of substance but in terms of function.

The first of the secondary pranas is called "forceful-movement" (Tib. *gyuwa*) and is associated with the visual organ. It helps us see things more clearly and has the quality or prana of water. The second prana is known as "continuous-movement" (Tib. *nampar gyuwa*) and ties in with the ear organ. This assists us to hear gross sounds, subtle sounds, and so on and it is the prana or element of wind. The third prana is called "thorough-movement" (Tib. *yangdakpar gyuwa*). It is connected to the nose organ and enables us to differentiate between smells—pleasant, unpleasant, gross, and subtle, in a similar way to how the previous one operates in terms of sound. This prana is connected to the earth prana element. The fourth one is known as "certain-movement" (Tib. *ngepar gyuwa*) and is connected to the organ of the body, which means the entire body. This allows us to distinguish between the different physical sensations—gross, subtle, pleasant, unpleasant, and so on. It is connected to the space prana element. The last one is called "complete-movement" (Tib. *raptu gyuwa*). This form of secondary prana has to do with the taste organ and is connected to the fire prana element. This helps us differentiate between different tastes—pleasant, unpleasant, gross, subtle, and so on.

So these are the five secondary pranas, which, as mentioned, are connected to the sensory organs. Until the age of 25 from the time of taking birth, these pranas help the individual grow and mature. From 25 years of age to 45, there is no change in prana. This is the period of preservation. The body has become fully mature and is maintained at a steady level. There is no growth of any kind and no added capacity occurs. From 45 years onwards, the prana begins to lose some of its power. It is said that if one is not working with the prana, gradually our breathing would become difficult. This is why as we get older, inhalation becomes more laborious. We experience a distinct difference in how efficiently we exhale and inhale.

How the pranas operate in relation to breathing is described as being masculine, feminine, or neutral. If one's breathing is harsh or coarse, it is described as "masculine," and if one is breathing slowly in a gentle fashion, it is called "feminine" prana. The neutral prana is described as "even."

In pranayama practice, we basically try not to breathe in a shallow way or too quickly. Breathing quickly is not seen in a positive light. The prana can be described as being either hot or cold, neither of which is considered to be a good thing. Hot prana or cold prana—sometimes referred to as "cool" prana—have to be balanced through pranayama.

Pranayama is practiced to prevent the diseases and conditions we have listed in relation to the five primary pranas and it also teaches us to breathe properly, since it is said that breathing improperly shortens one's life. So learning to breathe properly not only brings certain health benefits, but it also achieves longevity. One has to understand that, through pranayama, one is not simply working with the breath as we know it, when we inhale and exhale. We need to develop the understanding that prana is being expelled from our body through the openings of the eyes, ears, nose, mouth, and so on. In addition, we are sucking prana in from the outside through these openings and through the pores of our skin. So doing pranayama is not just working with the breath as we understand it, but we can also think of it as some kind of parallel to the normal process of breathing in oxygen. In this case, we are focusing on how to suck in prana and expel stale prana. As we exhale our stale breath and inhale fresh breath, this other process is occurring on a more subtle level as well.

It is said that on average, in a 24 hour period, we inhale and exhale 21,600 times or thereabouts. With pranayama, we are trying to approach that in a way that the rhythm of our breath becomes established, a pattern is established, so that there is no fluctuation or interruption in the steady flow of the breath. This has many benefits, not only physical benefits, which will be obvious, but benefits to the mind as well, which is of even more importance. This is because, as I explained earlier, mind and prana are intimately related.

Often, it is said that prana is the horse and mind is the rider, so that wherever mind goes, there is prana, and wherever prana goes, there is mind. If we work with the prana—especially when we have difficulties working with the mind—then we will be working with the mind as well. By working with the prana, our mind might become more manageable and stable, because the prana has become more stable. Many of the problems associated with mental agitation have to do with agitation on the pranic level.

Pranayama practice is not just for health but it has a spiritual goal and this is the main reason for practicing pranayama. One does pranayama so that the mind becomes less agitated and, by becoming calmer, it will become clearer. If our mind becomes clearer, we understand the mind better because mind's own nature is clarity. When the mind is not clear, this is because it is not working properly. It is not the case that this is just how mind is. If it is not working properly, that is not how it should be. Through pranayama practice and so on, we are actually causing the mind to work the way it should work, because that is how the mind is designed to be. Mind's nature is cognitivity.[38] That is its essential quality. Mind's essential quality is to cognize: to see, to perceive, to be aware. So if that is not happening, it is because the mind is not working properly and doing pranayama is helpful. As the teachings say, there is no doubt that it is beneficial so it is good to do it.

16
Tibetan Medicine

I spoke about pranayama in the previous chapter, and I will continue in relation to Buddhist ideas of disease and health, as it is discussed in the Tibetan Buddhist literature. I will not go into the history of the tradition, but the tradition itself is based on what are called the "Four Tantras." The general consensus seems to be that these tantras were put together by early Tibetan masters, rather than translated directly from Sanskrit treatises, although, of course, there are medical texts to be found in Sanskrit.

I will continue to speak about the idea of health, in relation to what are called the "three humors." When we are doing tantric practice, when we practice *lujong*—lujong simply means "training of the body"; *lojong* means "training of the mind"—this includes many kinds of *trulkhor* practices. Trulkhor means "Tibetan yoga" and pranayama is practiced in relation to trulkhor practices. Robert Thurman calls trulkhor "Tibetan technology," and actually it is a good translation because trulkhor does mean "technology." He says it is far superior to external technology, and he may be right. There are many different kinds of trulkhor practices. When you do trulkhor practices, the emphasis is on pranayama, but pranayama is also treated as one of the three humors in Tibetan Buddhist medical literature. There is prana vayu or wind prana, and then bile, and the third humor is phlegm. "Bile" is a translation of *tripa* in Tibetan; *peken* is translated as "phlegm." The idea is that if the wind or prana and the bile and phlegm, are working in harmony, then we can enjoy good health. If they are not in harmony, we will suffer physical ailments, illnesses, mental torment, and things of that kind.

Bile (Tib. Tripa)

As with prana, in Tibetan medical literature the bile is divided into five types. The various manifestations of bile perform different functions. The first one is called "digestive bile" (Tib. *juje*). It is located in the stomach and intestine and its function ranges in that area. As the name suggests, it helps with the digestive process but is also responsible for generating bodily heat. When this bile malfunctions, we end up with stomach and intestinal problems, loss of body heat, and so on.

The next type of bile function is known as "accomplishing bile" (Tib. *drupje*). *Drup* means "to accomplish or execute," and *je* means "agent," so it means: "something that executes or carries out a particular function." Its function lies in the heart region and it monitors our passions, emotions, and moods. It determines how we are feeling at any given time and it also has an impact on how much or how little sleep we are getting. When this function of bile is disrupted, various symptoms arise. As an example, we may begin to suffer from a lack of clarity in terms of our memory, and have problems recalling certain events from the past. Even on a daily basis, we may begin to become very foggy in the mind and be unable to think or see things clearly. We may also become very drowsy and lethargic, always wanting to sleep.

The third one has the name, "seeing bile" (Tib. *thongje*), which means the "bile function that allows us to see things." It lies predominantly in the visual organs. It is responsible for helping the visual organs operate at maximum capacity. If this function becomes disrupted then we can have symptoms indicating something is not working well, which can include the inability to bear sunlight, so too much light will hurt our eyes. We may even see white things as having a yellow tinge, like a person with jaundice.

Color-changing bile (Tib. *dangyur*) is the fourth category of functional bile. In Tibetan, *dang* means "color," *yur* means "change"—hence "change of color." This bile operates in the liver and its function is to regulate blood. It also assists in proper functioning of muscle tissue and things of that kind. The symptoms associated with malfunction of this form of bile include itchiness of the skin surface and yellowing of the skin. These are some examples but there are many other symptoms.

The last type is cleansing-complexion bile (Tib. *doksel*). *Dok* means "complexion" and *sel* means "to clear." As the name indicates, the function of this bile is to regulate one's complexion, to keep the skin texture and color in good condition, and so forth. Not surprisingly, the symptoms associated with malfunction of this bile involve the skin turning rough, craggy, and dry. In addition, the skin and the fingernails may darken, one may lose hair from the head and even the eyebrows may begin to thin out. This malfunction would cause one to become generally weak and deprived of energy.

Phlegm (Tib. Peken)

There are, again, five different types, when it comes to peken or phlegm. The first of them is supportive phlegm (Tib. *tenje*). *Ten* is "support" and *je* is "that which gives support." In each of these cases, the first in the set is the primary function, so tenje or supportive phlegm is the primary function of phlegm. This resides in the abdominal region. Its function is to regulate bodily fluid and also render support to the remaining four.

Both bile and phlegm have their functions and are much needed for our health and longevity, but they can also malfunction. With the supportive phlegm, when things go wrong we can expect to see a variety of symptoms. One malfunction would result in us losing our appetite and not feeling like eating, drinking, and so on. Instead, we may feel very nauseated and may throw up or vomit frequently but, instead of vomiting solid food, it would be liquid and sour-tasting. We could also expect to experience pain in the upper body and there may be a rise in temperature in the chest area. Symptoms like this may arise or be perceived.

The second one is mixed phlegm (Tib. *nyakje*). This means that in the stomach and intestine region, the function of this particular phlegm is to break down solid food and mix it into a semi-liquid state, in order to help with digestion. When this is not working very well, we begin to suffer from symptoms which would include poor digestion, tightness in the abdomen, accompanied by frequent belching, and vomiting.

The third type of phlegm, which assists us to taste or savor our eating experiences, *nyongje* in Tibetan, resides in the tongue. This third function of phlegm is responsible for helping us enjoy our food and being able to taste whether the foods we are eating are sweet, sour, tasty, bitter, astringent, or acrid. These are the standard flavors actually listed in Buddhist philosophical texts. Symptoms of dysfunction may be that our ability to fully savor or taste flavor is compromised and then our ability to distinguish tastes begins to wane. Not only that, but other symptoms may manifest, such as lack of thirst or a feeling of coldness in the tongue. Even one's voice may change and become rough or coarse.

The fourth kind of phlegm is *tsimje* in Tibetan. Tsim is "to be satisfied." The syllable, *je*, again, plays the role of a verb. This type means "something that brings satisfaction and enjoyment to our sensory inputs." This is located in the head. When we see something, smell something, taste something, or touch something, we get enjoyment, pleasure, from these experiences. We get satisfaction, as a result, but this type too may involve malfunction. Such symptoms may consist of visual distortion so we may not see an object in the correct proportions, color, or shape. Frequent sneezing may also be one of the symptoms, as may a feeling of heaviness on one side of the head. We may also frequently pick up influenza and colds.

The fifth and last one we call "connecting-phlegm" (Tib. *jorje*). The reason for that name is because this phlegm functions to allow the joints in our body to extend and contract, such as our legs, fingers, toes and so on. Normally, our joints are very flexible but this can degenerate and cause various symptoms, so that extending and retracting limbs becomes difficult and we develop problems with the joints. We might end up with arthritic problems, and swelling in the joints may also occur. Pain in the shoulders may also be a symptom.

Causes of Malfunction and Recommended Actions

Now, we may ask, "What causes the bile (Tib. *tripa*) and phlegm (Tib. *peken*) to malfunction?" To determine the cause, we need to look, first, at the psychological state; secondly, we have to view it from the perspective of the diet; and, thirdly, we should look at it from a behavioral point of view.

The psychological cause of bile problems actually comes, broadly, from anger, "anger" being a generic term associated with such things as bitterness, resentment, spite, and general unhappiness. This is the psychological reason for bile malfunction. The secondary reason might be injury to the gallbladder or eating too much spicy food, such as chili, eating food with a very strong sour taste or with too much salt in it, or food that is very greasy. So eating foods like this for a lengthy period of time can also contribute towards bile problems. Instead of including food like that in our diet, we should try to procure meat from animals raised in cold climates, such as beef, goat milk and butter, curd, and yoghurt.

Bile has two divisions, hot and cold, depending on whether it is heat-generated or cold-generated bile. Apart from dietary observations, we should also pay heed to our behavior and lifestyle. If we suffer from bile malfunction brought on by too much heat in the body, then we should not engage in much physical exertion; in fact we should not exercise at all. We should learn to monitor our angry behavior and pay attention to physical posture, how we are holding our body. Does the posture suggest anger or a feeling of being threatened? If so, we should try to spend more time in tranquil places, like gardens, especially those with water features, or sit by a riverbank, pond, or lake, trying always to sit in a cool place, a shady place with a cool breeze. All these things are helpful.

If the bile disorder is brought on by cold conditions, then we need to avoid sitting in cold, wet places and, when walking, we must do so in a very gentle fashion and not vigorously. We should make sure that we are not perspiring and that, when walking, we only continue to the point where we begin to perspire. It is recommended that we eat fresh butter from a cow or goat and eating fresh mutton or fish is also helpful. The food must always be fresh and cooked in a mild way with nothing too spicy included in the meal. Those are some brief guidelines and examples regarding bile.

It is said that phlegm (Tib. *peken*) malfunction is brought on by psychological bewilderment, where our mind is not very clear and in a state of confusion. In that context, we cannot think very clearly or make up our mind and are always unsure or uncertain about things. These are the psychological reasons why phlegm could malfunction. The secondary causes could involve diet and lifestyle. Consuming large quantities of food with an extremely bitter or sweet taste or eating very greasy foods, are all contributing factors to developing problems with phlegm. Another possible cause is that one may have become ill through eating unripe fruit, something that is not recommended. In addition, it is not healthy to lie down immediately after eating a full meal and this could contribute to the development of phlegm problems. In fact, overeating is one of the main causes of peken problems. Sleeping or taking a nap during the day as a habitual action may also be a cause of developing phlegm malfunction. If one swims in a cold river or spring during winter, for exercise, then that can also bring this about.

Instead of eating like that and leading that kind of lifestyle, one's diet should include mutton, fish, ground grains, and ginger tea. In terms of behavior, one should try to expose one's body to heat, to warmth, which would include activities such as spending time in the sun and doing lots of exercise, while making sure one is wearing warm clothing in cold conditions. These are helpful things and we should incorporate them into our life to deal with or prevent phlegm problems from arising.

These three humors have an impact on what are known as the "six hollow organs" and "five solid organs." The term "six hollow organs" refers to organs with cavities in them. They are the stomach, the large intestine, the gallbladder, the small intestine, the urinary bladder, and the sex organs, meaning both male and female. The five solid organs without cavities are the lungs, the heart, the liver, the spleen, and the kidneys.

The phlegm, bile, and prana impact on these organs. For example, in relation to the five solid organs, when phlegm impacts on the lungs in a negative way, the individual may feel that their chest is very full and may also feel dizziness. If phlegm impacts on the heart, they may experience lack of appetite and heaviness. If the liver is involved, they may feel pain in that organ after eating. If the spleen is affected, they will experience heaviness of breathing and a swollen or bulging abdomen. With the final one, the kidneys, there may be pain in the hips and a frequent urge to relieve themselves.

In that way, leading a healthy life has to do with a number of factors. It is not just about one aspect. Of course, medicinal remedies are also included as a measure for correcting health issues, but taking medicine is not the only answer. Rather, we try to look at our psychological state of mind, our diet and lifestyle, and at how we can relate to our environment. The other important point mentioned about the workings of phlegm is that the seasons also have an impact on how it functions and, in fact, on the functioning of all three humors.

We must be alert to these matters. The medical literature advises us to adapt our lifestyle so that what we do in summer, we do not do in winter, and what we do in winter, we do not do in autumn, in fall, and so on. We adapt according to our physical condition, whether one is a phlegm-dominated person, a bile-dominated person, or a wind or prana-dominated person. By taking this into account, we should try to create a lifestyle conducive to our health. This is in keeping with the Buddhist notion of seeing the interconnected nature of everything.

Good health is not to be had simply by following one particular diet, or doing physical exercise as our sole "healthy" activity, or merely engaging in a specific relaxation/stress-management regime. As it has been made clear, sometimes we need to stop exercising or reduce the amount we do and, at other times, we may have to exercise more. Exercise, alone, is not the answer for everyone or for even one person, and it is not the right thing to do to exercise in the same way, all year round. This has to be taken into account if we are to pursue a healthy lifestyle.

So Tibetan medicine is not just about taking medicine, but about living your life in a particular way so that you are mindful of both what you eat and of how you are living. I normally avoid using the word, but it is something of a "holistic" approach and it is very beneficial. If you are interested, you can further your studies and deepen your knowledge by discussing it with people who are expert in this area. I mentioned the connection between Tibetan medicine and pranayama. As I said, in the pranayama practices, the three humors are not really spoken about. More focus is on the pranayama itself but, if you look at it overall, the three humors—lung or vayu, bile and phlegm—have importance because they are fundamental to Tibetan medicine.

From a psychological point of view, lung is related to all things to do with desire, phlegm to all things to do with confusion, and bile to all things to do with anger.

Integral Approach to Health

Because of the way some people understand the Buddhist notion of renunciation, it may lead them to believe that even thinking about their health is a form of attachment or something like that. This is obviously not the case because if we enjoy robust health, then we will feel good in ourselves. If we feel good in ourselves, we will be more energetic, have a more positive outlook, and will therefore be of much more help to others. It will also become easier to work with others. If we are not feeling very good in ourselves, if we have too many worries and the body is not very strong, it may be difficult even to practice the Dharma. Even if one does not have robust health, if one is able to maintain the level of health one has by making the most of it, while still trying to improve it to the best of one's ability, all this is seen as very helpful.

We can also take an integral view in relation to the physical aspects and health and well-being. For instance, in terms of physical health, while relying on modern medicine, we could also be approaching our health issues in relation to alternative medicine and, particularly if we are involved in Buddhism, subtler forms of medicine.

In terms of how we approach the issue of health, then, of course, studying Western medicine, learning about modern medicine, is very important, but we need not be content with just that. We can go further and, from a Buddhist point of view, try to incorporate a more traditional approach to health and wellbeing, in addition to the modern approaches to health. Some of us may have a very one-sided approach, believing only in either modern medicine or another form of medicine. Of course, for certain conditions such as surgery, modern medicine cannot be beaten, however, it should be noted that the Buddhist view recognizes that alternative forms of medicine such as those we have been discussing, can help with chronic conditions.

In earlier periods of the development of Buddhism, the Buddhist tantric or esoteric masters incorporated the practices around them, even though they were not part of Buddhist practice. So, at that time, they were practicing the integral approach by integrating elements from other Indian traditions. Another example we can look at is that Tibetan tantric medicine contains *Ayurveda* where even the language is the same. This is traditional—it is part of traditional Buddhism. Even though Buddha did not necessarily talk about it that does not mean it is not traditional.

17
Conclusion

What "Integral Buddhism" means is that when we follow Buddhism, we look at all aspects of Buddhist teachings and practices and do not think of Buddhism purely as a philosophy, or as simply a tradition which promotes meditation, particularly mindfulness or tranquility meditation, for example. My intention has been to speak about Buddhism in a much broader sense, which is why I have addressed Buddhist philosophy, ethics, meditation, psychology, pranayama, Tibetan medicine, and even Western thought and science.

Integral Buddhism can be approached from many angles and perspectives, within one particular practice and tradition. The integral approach addresses many different levels and we say in Buddhism that no matter what it is that we attempt to incorporate into our Buddhist practice, it has to be encompassing, accommodating. That is the key point. The basic point at the core of the philosophy of integral Buddhism is the idea that whatever is useful for our growth, for our human prosperity, is something we need to pursue, no matter what it is.

Regardless of what our belief system is, in order to move forward it is inevitable that, in time, we will have to adapt. At the same time, however, we need to try to keep a balance, neither taking everything on board, nor throwing everything out that we might see as old or not modern enough. We try to retain that which we have inherited from tradition because there is much there that is still very relevant, extremely important, and which contains a potent message for the modern world. This is what we need to retain while, at the same time, being attentive to changing circumstances, social conditions, the political climate, and the natural environment.

Notes

SECTION 1: INTEGRAL BUDDHISM
Towards an Integral Buddhist View

1. Dharma and Buddhadharma are other terms for Buddhist teachings.

2. The 19th century Rimè (non-sectarian) movement, which was centered in East Tibet has played a major role in shaping modern Tibetan Buddhism. The Tibetan term "Rimè," meaning "unbiased" was adopted in the 19th century to express a non-sectarian approach within Tibetan Buddhism. The founders of this movement encouraged study and practice of all lineages in an unbiased fashion. They reaffirmed the different paths and lineages present in Tibet as valid and effective ways to enlightenment while encouraging study of a broad range of philosophical approaches. For a scholarly discussion of this movement see, *Rimè: Buddhism without prejudice*, Peter Oldmeadow, Shogam Publications (2012).

3. Jamgon Kongtrul Lodro Thaye (1813-99) was born in Kham, Tibet. A prominent Buddhist master of the Kagyu school, he was one of the founders of the Rimè movement of Tibetan Buddhism, along with Jamyang Khyentse Wangpo (1820-92), Chokgyur Lingpa (1829-70), and Patrul Rinpoche (1871-1927).

4. The concept of "*Path*" is extremely important in Buddhism, which places emphasis on our individual capacity to achieve liberation or enlightenment by ourselves, rather than relying on the power of another. When we embark on a journey, when we travel on the path, we must do so alone. No one can travel on the path for us, as nothing can replace first hand experience.

Enlightened practitioners (Buddhas and Bodhisattvas) provide guidance and information to assist a practitioner when embarking on a spiritual journey, or travelling on the path. This is an essential concept in the Buddhist tradition. The notion involved with the idea of travelling on the path is that even if one considers the insubstantial quality of all things, that does not mean there is no one travelling on the path. Rather, such considerations and contemplations are designed to build self-knowledge to help one become transformed from a state of delusion and confusion. By overcoming our delusions and confusion, we can gain insight into our own true nature and the nature of reality. Here, "insight" refers to developing a real understanding of ourselves and the phenomenal world. Through this understanding, our lives can become enriched. The path consists of working with ourselves so that gradually, by overcoming the various inhibitions, confusions, and delusions of mind, we start to develop more insight into our own true nature.

There are different methods used on the path to liberation and enlightenment. The *Shravaka* method aims to attain enlightenment for one's own sake. The other, the Bodhisattva approach seeks to gain enlightenment for the benefit of other beings. Both approaches are legitimate and the goal can be achieved from either perspective. Whichever approach is used, there are five stages of progress or development along the path that we travel: the path of preparation (also called the path of accumulation); the path of application; the path of seeing; the path of meditation; and the path of no more learning. These stages are designed to assist in the accumulation of wisdom and the development of love and compassion, to become a fully developed person. (*Essence Of Buddhism*, Traleg Kyabgon, pp 96-98, Shambhala Publications, 2001).

An Integral Approach to Meditation

5. Yana literally means "vehicle" and refers to the vehicle one is using on the path to enlightenment. The three yanas are Hinayana, or small vehicle, Mahayana, or large vehicle, and Vajrayana, or vehicle of indestructibility. All three vehicles can be used on one's path to liberation and enlightenment. Each shares an understanding of suffering and its causes, and assists us to overcome the causes of suffering through the use of meditation and other methods. The practitioner seeks to not only understand the causes of suffering—conflicting emotions such as jealousy and pride, and conceptual confusion, born of the belief that the self has enduring essence—but also to rectify the situation and overcome suffering.

   The Hinayana path has a vision or goal that is quite specific, and that is the wish to achieve liberation, enlightenment, or arhathood for oneself. Arhathood is a state in which one has rid oneself of the emotional conflicts of anger, jealousy, dissatisfaction, and so on. This approach does not have an emphasis of developing a compassionate and sensitive attitude as such, though such an attitude may be present or may develop. The Hinayanist is a type of practitioner with a particular self-oriented perspective. The Hinayanist hears and relates to the teachings on an intellectual level without fully practicing them or assimilating them. The Sanskrit term *shravakayana* is synonymous with Hinayana and means "vehicle of the hearers." The perspective of the Hinayana practitioner should not be confused with Theravada Buddhism, as is often the case. Theravada is a rich, ancient, and traditional school of Buddhism practiced in countries such as Sri Lanka, Thailand, and Vietnam. Hinayana is not determined by doctrine, school, or belief system, but by the internal attitude held by the practitioner in regard to their spiritual practice. This way of determining a given practitioner's status can also be applied to Mahayana and Vajrayana.

The Mahayana path has an expanded spiritual perspective, that of seeking to gain enlightenment for the benefit of others, and is known as the "path of purification" or the "Bodhisattvayana" or "Bodhisattva path." The Mahayanist's path requires the evolution of self-knowledge into wisdom, which is the mental transformation known as the "development of the mental aspect of buddha's being"—and development of the intention to help others into love and compassion, which is the physical transformation known as "developing the physical aspect of buddha's being." The development of both wisdom, through meditation, and compassion, through action and engagement in the world, is described as the two wings of a bird—both are required to help overcome the suffering of others. Such enriched and integrated self-development is designed to provide the Mahayana practitioner with the insight and skillful means to truly help others progress on the spiritual path. The Mahayana tradition has two aspects, the sutric and tantric traditions of Mahayana.

In Vajrayana, also known as Mantrayana, Tantrayana, and the path of transformation, the reference to *vajra*, which means "indestructible," relates to the indestructibility of one's buddha nature, one's true, primordially pure, untainted, fundamental nature. The word tantra means "continuity." Here, it references the continuation of the person's buddha nature on the spiritual path, thus the process of transformative purification does not suggest that the person becomes a different person. Rather, it refers to the coming together of the inner nature of the person within samsara, and the inner nature of the person when in a state of nirvana. That is to say, one's true nature is continuous but normally remains veiled behind delusions. As the delusion is purified, the true nature, the buddha nature is revealed. Thus the terms vajra, meaning "indestructibility," and tantra, meaning "continuity," can be seen as referring to the indestructible and continuous quality of buddha nature. Vajrayana is predominantly a path or process of transformation developed through the use of ritual practices, including visualization and mantra recitation.

6. The three principles of Buddhism are conduct, meditation, and wisdom.

7. *Anapanasati Sutta*, by Most Venerable "Bhante" Vimalaramsi Mahathera, Buddhist Association Of the United States, (2001) appears to have more information on this sutta.

8. Feelings can be regarded as physical sensations, as opposed to emotions such as anger or jealousy.

9. The four foundations of mindfulness are mindfulness of body, mindfulness of feelings, mindfulness of mind, and mindfulness of phenomena.

10. Asanga and Vasubandhu were brothers and major figures of the Yogacara or Vijnanavada school founded by them.

11. With Mahayana Buddhism, the altruistic aspect was brought to the fore, where it became more prominent than in early Buddhism, through the Mahayana ideal of the bodhisattva. A bodhisattva is a person who engages in compassionate activities with the intention of attaining enlightenment for the benefit of all living beings.

12. The text is available in English, along with Mipham Rinpoche's commentary. In Tibetan Buddhism, we use this text extensively because it is the only one that gives a succinct, but quite detailed description of how we should practice meditation. The other text used, but less frequently, is the meditation manual,

Bhavanakrama, by Kamalashila. His Holiness Dalai Lama has taught on this and a version is available in English. Bhavana is "meditation," *krama* means "stages," hence the Dalai Lama's book on this teaching is called *Stages of Meditation*. It is worth looking at those sources because Chandrakirti and Shantideva wrote on meditation, but there is no systematic presentation of meditation practices available. Shantideva devoted a chapter to meditation in *Bodhicaryavatara* and it takes the form of an extended meditation on the body, describing the stages of decay. It is seen as a very important meditation but there is no equivalent guide to such a practice presented in traditional Buddhist manuals.

13. In some esoteric, tantric, or Vajrayana Buddhist practices, traditional symbolic practices, including the visualizing of deities, are practiced. These deities are not necessarily considered to exist externally, but rather represent aspects of our true nature or enlightened mind.

Integral Buddhism, Ignorance, and Suffering

14. Pain and suffering are distinguished as different experiences here. Pain can be considered an unpleasant physical or mental sensation, whereas suffering arises as a response to not having recognized the true nature of reality. Traditionally, two causes of suffering are said to be the *kleshas* or conflicting emotions, and karma.

15. "Conflicting emotions" refer to what in Sanskrit are known as *kleshas*, mental phenomena considered to be negative and one of the causes of suffering. Examples of kleshas include ignorance, jealousy, anger, excessive desire, and so on.

16. Jung spoke about the shadow, meaning the aspect of ourselves that we do not want to acknowledge or go into—the alienated,

objectified, ignored. This according to Jung, in turn, begins to exert an influence on our normal day-to-day situations. That which is in the unconscious, floods into conscious experience. Jung, unlike Freud, talked about it in terms of "collective unconsciousness."

17. Examples of emotions include anger, sadness, joy, and so on, whereas feelings refer to sensations such as, for example, the feeling of the heart beating in the chest, sensations of heat and cold, or feelings of nausea in the stomach. These feelings may also accompany emotions.

18. Shantideva was an Indian monk and exponent of the Madhyamaka school. His text, *Bodhicaryavatara*, "A Guide to the Bodhisattva's Way of Life," is an important Mahayana Buddhist text.

The Integral Approach to Overcoming Suffering

19. In this context, Rinpoche defines feelings as predominately physical sensations. Emotion is the result of our thinking processes and habitual responses. As with pain and suffering, emotions and feelings coexist, as there are corresponding physical sensations that accompany most emotions. For example, the emotion of anger is often accompanied by physical sensations such as raised temperature, accelerated pulse, and a quickening of the breath, etcetera.

20. The relative level is the level of reality dependent on interpretation and the subjective states of the individual, and only true within the conventional framework of one's own experience. Ultimate reality, or emptiness, refers to the insubstantial nature, or lack of inherent existence, of all phenomena.

21. Singing and pranayama can be seen as being under the category

of both body and speech.

22. As a result of our habitual tendencies, karmic traces and dispositions are left in the storehouse consciousness, the *alayavijnana*.

Working with Suffering and Becoming Stronger

23. There are degrees of enlightenment and before we attain perfect Buddhahood, we can still make an effort to become more enlightened. In other words, we can learn to elevate ourselves. This term "elevation," (Skt. *arya*; Tib. *pakpa*), has the connotation of lifting ourselves above the state of confusion or ignorance that we are in as ordinary human beings, before having discovered the Dharma and embarked on the path.

24. In Mahayana Buddhism, a bodhisattva has the wish to benefit all sentient beings and works for their enlightenment.

25. Chenrezig (Skt. *Avalokiteshvara*) represents the embodiment of love and compassion in Mahayana Buddhism.

Foundations of Wisdom

26. Atma or Atman: The Buddhist approach to the human mind is what is called "non-essentialist" or "non-substantialist," *anatman* (Skt.). At the time the Buddha taught, Hindu philosophers and spiritual masters spoke about substances. They taught that the world is unreal but that Brahma has substance and inherently exists so is therefore substantial, and that through contemplation, mental processes are revealed as temporary, but that there is something that is stable, permanent, eternal. They called it Atma or soul.

27. Supervenience is a term in philosophy used to describe where the lower level features of a system determine the upper level features.

Abhidharma (Pali: Abhidhamma)

28. Shakyamuni Buddha also known as Gautama Buddha, was born "Siddhartha Gautama" into a royal family and lived between 563 and 483 BCE.

29. A monad is a philosophical term adopted at one point by the philosopher Gottfried Wilhelm Leibniz, who referenced the monad as an elementary particle.

30. Mind-Training of Mahayana Buddhism.

Madhyamaka

31. The fourth of the five skandhas is samskara, translated as "formations, conditioned factors, or dispositions." Skandhas or aggregates are the different elements that make up the self. The five skandhas are form (Skt: *rupa*); feeling (Skt: *vedana*); perception (Skt: *samjna*); dispositions (Skt: *samskara*); and consciousness (Skt: *vijnana*).

12. Madhyamaka, Emptiness, and Compassion

32. Heinrich Dumoulin, a Jesuit scholar of Zen Buddhism, has written many books on Zen Buddhism, in one of which he says that the ideas of emptiness and compassion are incompatible.

33. Buddhist deities.

SECTION 3: PSYCHOLOGY

Psychology, Spirituality, and the Mind

34. The two fundamental kinds of meditation. Shamatha meditation is tranquility meditation or calm abiding, and vipashyana meditation is insight meditation, which involves insight into reality.

SECTION 4: HEALTH AND WELL-BEING

Prana and Pranayama

35. Prana is Sanskrit for "psychophysical energy." Pranayama involves breathing exercises that work with prana, the psychophysical energy pathways (Skt: *nadi*), and the psychophysical energy centers (Skt: *chakras*).

36. A sadhana is a spiritual practice used in tantric Buddhism, involving chanting, prayers, visualization, singing, offerings, and meditation.

37. A contraction of Tib. *me dang mnyam par gnas pa*.

38. "Cognitivity" relates to cognition and the mental processes of knowing, perception, and so forth.

Index

Abhidharma 78–81, 88, 98, 100, 115–116, 121
Acceptance 124–125, 127, 129, 136
Alayavijnana 89–90
All-permeating prana 144
Apana vayu 149
Arupakaya 107
Arya 46
Asanga 14, 88, 90, 139
Asvabhava 95, 102
Atisha 83–84
Atman 70
Attraction 65, 126
Avadhuti 148
Avatamsakasutra 105
Aversion 31, 65, 126

Bile 155–157, 159–163
Bodhicitta 85, 104–106, 108, 110–111, 113
Bodhisattva 84, 104–106, 108, 110–111, 113
Body 1, 8–9, 12–13, 16–17, 19–20, 23, 28, 38–40, 44, 52, 59, 61–62, 64–65, 78, 93, 107, 120, 139–140, 142–148, 150–152, 155–156, 158–161, 163
Body, speech, and mind 52, 61–62, 139
Breath xv, 8–12, 19–20, 38, 44, 146, 152–153
Buddha 7–8, 10–14, 2–22, 26, 39, 47–49, 51, 53–55, 57, 59–66, 70–73, 78–79, 81–82, 104, 107, 111, 164

Causes and conditions 65–66, 70–72, 95–97, 102–103, 112, 120
Chakra 140–142, 144, 149, 150
Chögyam Trungpa 132, 135
Cold 116, 142, 144, 152, 159–161
Compassion 8, 98, 100–101, 107–110, 112, 114–115
Conceptualization 34
Conditioning 101
Consciousness 9, 15, 66, 82, 89, 150
Craving 47–48, 50–53, 56, 59, 63–66, 68, 103
Crazy wisdom 132, 135

Desire 47–48, 50–51, 56, 63–66,
Detachment 42–43, 48
Dharmakaya 39
Dharmas 64, 72, 79–81, 108, 114–117
Downward-moving prana 142
Dzogchen 20, 132–133, 135–136

Ego 26, 37, 49, 53, 100, 102
Egolessness 53, 56
Emotions 10–11, 13, 22, 24, 27, 31, 37, 44, 47–50, 52–53, 55–56, 63–64, 67, 69–70, 80–81, 89, 96–97, 100–102, 106, 113, 115, 120–125, 127, 131, 136–137, 140, 146–147,

156
Emptiness 20, 76, 82, 91–95, 98–104, 106–108, 116–117
Enlightenment 6, 33, 53–55, 58, 83–85, 106, 117, 138
Eternalism 41, 70, 83, 102
Ethics 28–29, 31, 66, 70, 73, 119–121, 165
Exercise xv, 15–17, 25–26, 28, 59–60, 75, 88, 106, 113, 143, 145, 150, 160–162

Five Primary Pranas 149, 151
Five Secondary Pranas 149, 151–152
Fixation 68, 96–97, 103–104,
Food 30, 150, 157–160
Four noble truths 28, 45–46

Generosity 107, 112–113
Gyengyu 149–150
Gyuwa 151

Happiness 7, 49, 55–56, 112, 125
Health 1, 3, 15, 25, 52, 64, 93, 138, 140, 144–145, 152–153, 155–157, 161–163
Heat 142–143, 145, 156, 159, 161
Hinayana 14, 83–85

Ignorance 2, 21–24, 47, 50, 63, 65, 79, 126
Inherent existence 82, 95, 97–102, 104, 116–117
Integral Buddhism xv, 1, 4, 20–21, 42, 117, 165
Interdependent origination 69–71, 100

Kadampa 84
Karma 40, 58, 70–73, 81, 97

Khyapje 149
Lalana 148
Logic 43, 80, 98, 117
Madhyamaka 93–94, 98–99, 115–116
Mahamudra 20, 132–133, 135–136
Mahayana Buddhism 19, 31, 39, 54, 62, 78–79, 105, 107–108, 112, 115
Meditation xv, 2–3, 6–11, 13–17, 19–20, 24, 26, 29–30, 32, 38, 44, 54–56, 61, 64–65, 67, 74, 88–89, 120, 122, 131, 136, 165
Meditative concentration 56, 112, 114
Merit 2, 52, 60, 106
Mind 1, 3, 7–11, 16–18, 20, 22, 31, 35, 38–40, 43–44, 52–53, 55, 60–64, 66–67, 75, 77, 80–81, 85, 87–94, 96, 100, 105, 107, 110–111, 115–117, 119–123, 127, 131–132, 135–137, 139–140, 144, 146–147, 149–150, 153–156, 160–161
Mindfulness 2, 11–14, 18, 20, 28, 44, 58, 60–61, 69–70, 113, 120, 122, 135, 165
Moral precepts 107, 112, 119
Morality 29, 70, 73, 91, 112, 118

Nadi 19, 144, 147–148
Nagarjuna 92–105, 115, 139
Nampar gyuwa 151
Neyartha 105–106
Ngepar gyuwa 151
Nihilism 41, 70, 95, 102

Nirvana 6, 33, 53, 107
Nitartha 105
Noble eightfold path 58–59
Nyamnge 149

Pain 13, 21, 33–34, 45, 56, 58, 158–159, 161
Paramitas 110–112
Past 71–73, 82, 123, 156
Patience 107, 112–114
Philosophy xv–xvi, 1-2, 24–25, 27, 30, 58, 65, 68, 74–77, 87–88, 94, 96, 98, 115–118, 138–139, 165
Phlegm 155, 157–163
Pleasure 13, 49, 131, 141, 158
Prajnaparamita Sutra 98, 105
Prana 9, 19, 138, 140, 142, 144, 146–153, 155–156, 161–162
Prana vayu 149, 155
Pranayama 17, 38, 138–142, 145–147, 149, 152–155, 162, 155
Prapanca 147
Pratityasamutpada see Interdependent origination
Present 9–11, 13, 71–73, 82, 129
Psychology xv, 1–2, 24–25, 30, 44, 74, 117–121, 124–126, 129, 131–132, 135–137, 165
Pudgalavadins 82–83

Raptu gyuwa 151
Rashana 148
Reality 2, 13, 37–38, 47, 53, 68–70, 76–77, 79–80, 83, 87–91, 94, 97, 99, 103, 105, 115–117, 168, 172, 176
Relative reality 80, 90–91
Renunciation 42–43, 48, 163
Rupakaya 107

Saddhara Pundarika Sutra 105
Samana vayu 149
Samsara 22, 24, 46, 50, 99, 106–107, 171
Sarvastivada 82–83, 85–86, 100
Science xv, 2, 117, 165
Self 14, 23–27, 32, 37, 38, 40, 50–51, 53, 56–57, 63–64, 70, 82, 100–102, 124, 130–131, 133
Self-identity 51
Sense organs 66, 151
Shamatha 122–123, 175
Shantideva 31, 106, 110, 114, 172–173
Soklung 149
Spirituality 1–2, 39, 132–136
Strength 25, 56–57
Suffering 21–22, 26–29, 33–36, 38, 40–42, 44–47, 50–51, 53, 57–59, 61, 63, 65, 69, 72, 79, 103–104, 112–113, 169–170, 172–173
Svabhava 82, 94, 97–98, 100, 102–103

Tantra 139–140
Tantrayana see Vajrayana
Theravada 16, 83, 85
Thinking 2–3, 9–11, 15, 23, 26–27, 30, 35–36, 40, 43–45, 49–50, 53, 56–57, 66, 69–70, 75–76, 92–93, 100–104, 107, 110, 115–118, 121–124, 128, 130–131, 133–135, 140–141, 147, 149, 163
Three Humors 155, 161–162
Thursel 149
Tibetan Medicine 73, 155, 162–163, 165

Transformation 39, 54, 56, 170
Trulkhor 155

Udana vayu 149
Ultimate reality 90, 174
Upward-moving or ascending prana 142, 150, 149

Vajrayana Buddhism 138–139, 169–172
Vasubhandu 88, 139
Vayu 149, 155, 163
Vigor 17, 44, 107–108, 112–114
Vijnanavadin see Yogacara
Vipashyana 122–123, 176

Vyana vayu 149

Western Medicine 163
Western Philosophy 30, 87
Wind see Vayu
Wisdom xv, 7, 32, 50, 52–53, 59, 63–64, 67, 70, 73, 100, 107, 109–110, 112, 114–115, 123, 132, 135

Yangdakpar gyuwa 151
Yoga xv, 1, 19, 38, 61, 73, 88, 139, 155
Yogacara 87–88, 115–117

Zen Buddhism 74, 132, 175

www.ingramcontent.com/pod-product-compliance
Lightning Source LLC
Chambersburg PA
CBHW071918290426
44110CB00013B/1396